FENECH

THE OFFICIAL

BIOGRAPHY

Lester-Townsend Publishing

For Paul Fenech, a real fighter, and to dead end kids
everywhere looking for a way out.

FENECH

THE OFFICIAL

BIOGRAPHY

by

GRANTLEE KIEZA
and
PETER MUSZKAT

Lester-Townsend Publishing Pty. Ltd.
Sydney

Published in 1988 by Lester-Townsend Publishing
Pty. Ltd.   5 Glenmore Rd., Paddington. 2021. NSW.

National Library of Australia
Cataloguing-in-Publication data
  Kieza, Grantlee, Fenech, The Official Biography

   ISBN 0 949853 15 1

   1. Fenech, Jeff. 2. Boxers (Sports) — Australia
— Biography. I. Muszkat, Peter. II. Title.

796.8'3'0924

Printed by Globe Press, Pty. Ltd. Melbourne.

Contents

Introduction

Jeff Fenech became an Australian hero because of an intense will to win. At a time when Australia was struggling on the world sporting scene, he became something of a great warrior . . . a kid from the back streets of Marrickville who took on the best fighters the world could offer and beat them all.

As an amateur he missed out on an Olympic gold medal because of a controversial decision. Less than 200 days after turning professional he was a world champion. By 1988, he had become one of only 11 men in boxing history to hold three world titles.

Despite his rapid rise to fame and fortune, his ascent into the record books and a millionaire's neighbourhood, did not come smoothly. His family was constantly burdened with problems — sickness, death and no money. Fenech fought with his brothers, he fought with gang rivals, he fought with Olympic officials, he even fought with the man who moulded his destiny.

Fenech was good at one thing — fighting. He was the cunning streetfighter heading for a life of crime. When he walked into the Newtown Police Youth Club one day, his life changed. He could fight all he wanted — this time legally and with the complete blessing of the law. Under the guidance of trainer Johnny Lewis, Fenech, at almost breakneck speed, in boxing terms, took on the world — and won.

This is Jeff Fenech's story. A true story of a street kid who made it to the top of the world — with a little help from his friends, and with a lot of guts and determination.

1
Life On The Run

"Prizefighting offers a profession to men who might otherwise commit murder in the street"
Norman Mailer, US writer.

Running, running again. He was always running. The sounds of his stolen sandshoes slapping against the bitumen of a dead end street.

He was frightened and alone. His mate Raymond was having his face kicked in by a taxi driver who didn't like being taken for a ride. Especially when there was no money for the fare and only two punks laughing at his sweaty, red-faced indignation.

Jeff Fenech was always running. His adolescence was spent on the road and in the alley ways of the tough neighbourhoods where he learnt to steal and fight and where the chase was his way of getting money for nothing and kicks for free.

It doesn't take a master criminal to rob a taxi driver. And nobody ever accused Jeff Fenech of being a Professor Moriarty, or even a Ronald Biggs. He was just a bored brat who couldn't care less if some cabbie's family went hungry that night. The chase meant everything to him.

"To get chased was a way of getting excitement, to relieve boredom," Fenech says. "I hated school. I got expelled from one and the teachers hated me wherever I went. I didn't care about schoolwork. And I was as stubborn as hell. We used to pinch the money from cabbies all the time. Two of us would jump in the cab, get him to drive us somewhere and then jump out and do the bolt.

"We'd split up and when he went after one bloke the other one would go back to the cab and grab the cash. Usually they hid it behind the sun visor or under the seat. You didn't have to search too hard to find a fat little wad of bills.

"It wasn't so much the money even. We never really

thought about what getting robbed would do to a cab driver or what knocking off milk money for chocolates or newspapers or books would do to the shop owners. We just thought about ourselves. It was selfish. But in this world if you want something you go and get it the best way you can. I liked to fight and steal. I never liked to work all that much.

"Getting chased by cab drivers was also a good way to stop being bored."

But it was also a good way to get hurt. Especially when the cab driver couldn't take a joke or a loss in pay.

"One time me and Raymond did the bolt on a cabbie and he didn't take it too well. He hunted us down in his car. Me and Raymond were running for our lives. Really. The bloke wanted to kill us dead for sure."

Down one side street. Up a lane. Headlights stabbing at the boys' backs as their feet echoed through the night and as mongrels barked and a cabbie swore to get even.

Two young thieves running to save their necks. The adrenalin pumped. Just like a real dirty street fight. Lungs burned and the sweat oozed down the skin.

A dead end street. A speeding car behind them. A frantic driver turned into a maniac. Fear. Excitement. The chase. Raymond splits to the left. Jeff jumps a fence. The cab screeches to a halt. The cabbie bursts from his cab like a cannonball.

"I'll kill you. I'll kill you. I'll tear out your heart."

Fenech runs and runs. Seconds tick away as his heart starts to burst. He ducks through backyards. He steals his way over rubbish bins and children's toys. His eyes and ears wait for danger.

But he hears nothing like the voice of a killer cabbie. He keeps to the shadows of the back streets. He avoids the street lamps. He hears a husband and wife quarrelling and the thud of a punch. A moan. He slows at last.

He hears cars glide past. He sees a cab and his heart rate quickens for a flash. But the taxi passes.

Soon his trot has slowed to a walk. And then a saunter. The feeling in his legs comes back. He is in St Peters. He looks for the faces of his friends and brothers. He sees Raymond hunched on his front steps.

He sees Raymond's face covered with blood. He jumps out of eyesight. He sees the police. They don't see him. He makes it home to lie to his father. To lie to his mother. To boast to his brothers. And to plan his next big chase.

"That kind of thing happened all the time," Fenech admits, "I didn't like sitting around home doing nothing."

Fenech's brother Henry says: "Jeff was a wild kid. I guess we all were really. He was always in fights and he would always make sure he won. Even at school he knew who he could beat and who he couldn't beat. He was always smart. Street smart. And he was always tough and ruthless. I've still got the scar where he stabbed me in the leg with a compass."

Fenech's sister and great fan Mrs Rita Adamo says the street fights, the gangs and tough times were all catalysts for an iron will which her brother would forge in his future boxing career. A will that would allow him to ignore pain, accept sacrifice and wonder what the hell tiredness felt like in his most memorable bouts.

"Jeff was always a winner," she says proudly. "He always was in love with physical fitness and the idea of physical perfection. He always wanted to be the fittest, toughest, strongest man on earth. In a way that's what he became as a world boxing champion. There's probably no fitter boxer in the world than J and for mental and physical strength an opponent has never come close to him.

"It was the same when he was a kid at home. He couldn't bare to lose at anything. Marbles, fights, cards, a running race. You name it and J would drive himself like a fanatic to win at everything."

From as early as anyone can remember, Fenech has followed the same creed as Red Sanders, the American college football coach, who, in 1940, was the first to quip the immortal line: "Winning is not everything, it's the only thing."

No one will ever know the precise moment when Jeff Fenech went from being just another street kid, to what his trainer John Lewis would so often describe him as: "A dead set winner".

Maybe it was in the middle of an intense and grisly brawl at the speedway one night when representing the honour of the Newtown Hoods. Maybe it was playing hooker for Newtown in a Sydney rugby league competition when a rival player headbutted him and Fenech decided to get his own back and then some.

Maybe it was one morning when he hid in a corner of a supermarket and ate a breakfast of chocolates while his mother cleaned someone's floor and he dodged the shop assistants who always wondered why the clean little kid who came in every day always left with a grubby face.

Or maybe it was running down a dead end street with his friend Raymond and promising himself that one day he would have all the excitement and adventure of the chase without having to hide because of it.

Certainly the bond Fenech would make with his trainer Johnny Lewis when he started boxing helped in the evolution of a resolve and determination that may only be matched in sport today by that of Iron Mike Tyson, the juvenile juggernaut and heavyweight champion who fights for himself as much as he does for his late, great mentor, Cus D'Amato.

Fenech drew strength from loyalty long before he became an amateur boxer. The Newtown Police Boys Club, where he was introduced to boxing, only channelled his vision, only gave him a specific goal.

"If he has one characteristic that dwarfs all others," wrote Greg Hunter in Penthouse magazine, "It is his extreme loyalty. Not unlike many other children of migrant families, he has embraced what he imagines to be the essence of true blue Australianess with religious fervour."

The bonds Fenech first made as a juvenile thug contributed to the astonishing mental powers he would develop at a young age.

Fenech has a lot in common with gridiron coaches. One of the greatest, Vince Lombardi, once said: "Nobody is hurt. Hurt is your mind. If you can walk, you can run." Fenech, who has been playing mind games all his life, couldn't agree more.

"I'm lucky in the way that I can switch off, from whatever is happening around me whenever I want to," Fenech says, "In street fights I learnt to ignore the pain. If someone was trying to smash my face in, I would just concentrate on beating him instead. And I always came through.

"In boxing, my belief in John Lewis and the strength he gives me with his love makes me all that tougher in the mind. Whenever I'm hurt or whenever I find it hard to breathe, I tell myself to keep going. I tell myself that there's no way my fitness will let me down."

"Jeffrey has always been very smart," says brother-in-law Mick Adamo. "He doesn't let anybody or anything run his life. He's always done what he wanted to do. And he's always had the guts and the brains to do it. When he was a kid he wouldn't let anybody stand over him. In boxing it's the same thing. They're out to get his title. And he'll die before he lets them."

The iron will that would see Fenech leave boxing in a coffin rather than lose is a state of mind that all athletes aspire to, but few attain.

It has its origins in many areas of a complex street kid and world-famous athlete, part boy, part vicious animal, part businessman, part hustler. A friend to love and an enemy to fear and loathe.

It is also the single most admirable facet of the Fenech phenomena.

"There is no need to ponder what psychic paradox gives rise to the hero worship Australians bestow on him," writes Greg Hunter. "There is no mystery about it. Everyone who has seen him fight knows that Jeff Fenech's triumph is a triumph of the will, of that righteous stuff embodied in men like rugby league international Tommy Raudonikis and John Sattler and Wayne Pearce and a host of others but in no one so much as it is in Jeff Fenech."

Like Rocky Marciano, the late, great heavyweight of the 1950s, with whom he has often been compared, Fenech's strength has always been his strength — physical and mental. Marciano beat men with his will. No matter how many punches they blocked, he threw more. Until they could no longer hold him off. Until they could no longer prevent the triumph of a stronger mind.

Until he was 17 years old Fenech was a tough young man trapped in a world of dead end streets. At 17 he found an escape.

The champion's champion Sugar Ray Robinson once said: "I ain't never liked violence".

Jeff Fenech said: "I like a bit of violence. I make it work for me".

And Fenech still loves the chase. Only in boxing it's the other guy who ends up running away. ■

2
A Fighting Start

*"Most of my friends in the ghetto was into
dope or playing gangsters or getting killed up.
A guy named Chucky got shot dead in the
head three times and Ambro, the biggest fat
boy in the street, was found dead with a
needle in his arm. All I knowed was that I had
to get out."*

Leon Spinks, heavyweight champion.

Marrickville is not a pretty place. The working class centre of Sydney's bustling inner-west is a sprawling mosaic. Black smoke, grey factories, red rooftops. It's hard to believe that only a 20-minute drive away, the waters of the world's most spectacular harbour lap against some of the most precious real estate in either hemisphere.

But Marrickville's huge mansions, decaying relics of a time when it was one of the more fashionable parts of colonial Sydney, now mingle uneasily with the smoke-stacks and the trucks that snarl its narrow streets. And the breath-taking splendour of those harbour foreshores and ocean beaches might just as well be on another planet.

Marrickville is Jeff Fenech territory. Typical fighting territory. Exactly the sort of place where a young kid of battling Maltese migrants had to grow up if he wanted to be a boxing champion. Tough, bleak, uncompromising. It's true that hungry fighters make the best fighters. Jeff Fenech liked to be a hungry fighter even though he really didn't need to be one. As the youngest of six kids he was spoiled beyond the family's means. But many of his pals weren't too sure where their next sandwich was coming from and young Fenech, like them, seemed to enjoy living on the precipice. He revelled in the uncertainties of poverty even though his family was no poorer, no more deprived than many others in their neighbourhood.

There is a common myth that Fenech is the slum kid who

grew up fighting for his shirt and who used the talents he needed to survive on the street to punch his way to the Olympic Games and world professional titles. In truth, Fenech was a violent street hoodlum, who gravitated toward petty theft and serious assault because he lacked parental control or any feelings of remorse toward his victims. His only remorse was getting caught.

Fenech learnt to fight young. "I started stealing things and bashing people when my Dad was in hospital with his bad heart," Fenech recalls. "My Mum was always visiting him or out working to feed us. I could pretty much do what I wanted to. I've never felt guilty for hurting someone or taking their money. It's the same thing in the boxing ring. I wish I could have bashed Shingaki more and I wish I could have really hurt Jerome Coffee. That way they'd have never wanted to fight me again."

Most of the people work hard unless they're on social security benefits. Marrickville might not be a slum nor a ghetto, but it's still the kind of place from where its youth craves to break out. The kind of place where teenagers with nothing on their minds, but trouble, congregate in the main streets and look for an outlet for their frustrations. The kind of place where street brutality and wailing sirens hardly turn a head.

Jeff Fenech grew up in Marrickville and nearby Newtown, St Peters, Sydenham and Enmore. Not the most picturesque or fashionable parts of Sydney, but a likely nursery for a world boxing champion.

While Fenech now owns a waterfront home in Sydney and a three-storey house on the picturesque Central Coast near Gosford, he still spends time in Marrickville. Old habits die hard. He enjoys the surroundings where he is most familiar. In just 12 months and with a sympathetic public commiserating with him over the controversial Olympic defeat in Los Angeles, he was transformed from a struggling and little-known club fighter to a world professional champion, Australian athlete of the year. He drives his flashy Maserati sports car through the streets where he was once feared and now admired. He points out the ovals where his killer instinct was honed on the football field, the roof tops where his pre-teen friends once made startling daylight plunders, the street corners where he once fought for kicks.

"Over there's where I led the Boys Home team against the Catholic Brothers," he says. "They led 17-0 at half-time but we came back to just get done 17-16. After that we robbed their tuck shop and had a great party on the way home."

Next to the Marrickville Hotel where life-size cardboard cut-outs of the Marrickville Mauler advertise Carlton 2.1 beer, the multi-lingual medical centre confirms the ethnic mix. It's the same across the street.

There's the Andy Palumbo real estate office, the Van Hung butcher, Corinthian Restaurant, the My-Tin Vietnamese jewellery store, Hai-yen Viet-Chinese cafe, a Greek photographic studio and the Marrickville Drive-In liquor cellars where Fenech again proudly recommends the merits of his sponsor's brew.

It was against this cosmopolitan backdrop that Paul and Mary Fenech came to the Marrickville area 23 years ago.

It's been a rocky road for Jeff Fenech. With his gang he's walked tall down some mean streets and fled like a frightened animal down others.

Marrickville, the suburb he and his mates once terrorised, is now proud to call him its own. They hold civic receptions and parade him through the streets as a conquering hero.

And the Marrickville Hotel, one of his first sponsors, does a roaring trade.

Fenech liked to run with petty crims and juvenile delinquents. He liked to be the boss and the "brains" of the gang. Street kids spoke his language. In Marrickville he had every chance to learn the violent trade that made him a common name on police files — the same violent trade that would make him a hero and idol to millions. He learnt to fight hard for what was his and what belonged to others. Boxers who start their lives without a prevailing sense of humanity are usually the best.

Joyce Carol Oates, an American writer, said in her book, *On Boxing*, that traditionally the sport was credited with changing the lives of ghetto-born or otherwise impoverished youths who, like the '50s heavyweight contender Tommy Jackson, fought "'cos there's nothin' else" they could do.

"It is impossible to gauge how many boxers have in fact risen from such beginnings," she said. "But one might guess it to be about 99 per cent — at the present time."

One of the standard arguments for not abolishing boxing is that it provides an outlet for the rage of under privileged youth who can make lives for themselves by way of fighting one another instead of fighting society.

And in boxing Fenech realised he could become admired for the very same traits that as a youth, he was condemned. In boxing, values are different.

"Here we find ourselves through the looking glass," Oates said. "Values are reversed, evaginated; a boxer is valued not for his humanity but for being a killer, a hit man, an animal, for being savage, merciless, devastating, ferocious, vicious, murderous. Opponents are not merely defeated as in a game, but are decked, stiffed, starched, iced, destroyed, annihilated.

"Much of the appeal of Roberto Duran for intellectual boxing aficionados . . . was that he seemed truly to want to kill his opponents: in his prime he was the baby-faced assassin with the dead eyes and deadpan expression."

Fenech was never a hungry fighter. He just pretended to be. He spent hours in front of his video cassette recorder, watching the exploits of Rocky Balboa, copying the man's daring, dauntlessness, virility, fearlessness — the very essence of Rocky's masculinity. He framed posters of Sylvester Stallone and hung them in 3-D around his bedroom. Sometimes he would lie there for hours, hands behind his head, his eyes flickering from one to the other. He would jog through the back streets of Marrickville, face hooded the way Balboa did. And on fight nights he would walk to the ring, his forehead bowed on the shoulder of his trainer — a routine copied from Stallone and Rocky co-star Burgess Meredith.

With a little help from the movies, Fenech's is the classic Rocky story of Australia in real life. An undisciplined and bored young thug who bashed his way to a boys' home, then to fame and fortune before his 21st birthday. A cheat, a liar, a thief and later a national hero.

There has hardly ever been a worthwhile fighter born into affluent surroundings. Certainly not Jeff Fenech. Marrickville is an officially "disadvantaged" suburb. Not the pits, but still a few notches below underprivileged. It's a place where belching chimney smoke meets irritating exhaust fumes from the trucks that roar through its streets. The kind of place where aeroplanes flying in and out of nearby Mascot come so close to the ground you think they're about to crash into your lap.■

3
A Winner's Heart

"Life is the best left hooker I ever saw . . . "
Ernest Hemingway, US writer.

The first time Paul Fenech realised he had heart disease was the night he dropped dead. He was 32 years old, a Maltese-born storeman living with his pregnant wife and their five children in a crummy, rented shack at Pyrmont, a dockside Sydney suburb.

Paul Fenech died that night in 1964 and went straight to hell, a living hell he endured for 24 years. He had so many birthdays in nearby Royal Prince Alfred Hospital, the nurses spent a small fortune on birthday cakes and candles. When he spoke, his words were punctuated by the constant, precise ticking of the pacemaker that kept him alive.

He had been walking up the stairs at home when his heart first gave out.

"I was dead," he would exclaim, happy to tell everyone more than two decades after the event. "I dropped dead on the spot. My ticker just stopped beating.

"But God knows, when I hit that top step my heart must have started to beat again. The shock of it. I rolled down the steps, bumping my head and arms and legs and everything else on the way down, but by the time I got to the bottom I was alive. There were cuts and bruises and blood everywhere. But I was alive."

Paul Fenech died for the last time on Sunday, May 29, 1988, one day after Jeff's 24th birthday. After years of misery and pain, he died a happy man.

The patriarch of the Marrickville Fenechs, Paul was a fiercely proud man with wavy silver hair and an olive glow to his skin that belied the grave illnesses he survived. He came to Australia in 1951 and the following year married Mary

Aquilina who had migrated from Malta only a matter of months after Paul had gone looking for a better life.

Their first child died in the womb. Mary had been hurrying out the gate from their home when it slammed shut on her swollen belly. By 1964 and five healthy babies later, she was pregnant with the future world champion when her husband came home early from his night shift, complaining of chest pains and shortness of breath.

It was late evening and the waves lapped gently against the freighters docked at the Pyrmont wharves.

"I heard Paul come in and I asked him to go check on the kids," Mary remembers.

"I thought they were all asleep but with five little ones, who knows what they could have been doing? I heard Paul walking up the stairs and the next thing, I heard him coming down. End over end. Bump, Bump, Bump."

So began 24 years of torture for Paul Fenech. Torture that would force Mary to leave her children at home and trek a continuous loop between her job as a cleaning woman, the hospitals where her husband more often than not hovered between life and death, and the home they had moved to in Florence St, St Peters, where her children would have to fend for themselves and where her baby Jeffrey was starting to discover that life without grown-ups was a licence for belting up other kids and pinching their toys.

"Paul would be in hospital for three months, six months. He was always in there," said Mary.

"I would stay in hospital with Paul every night. When he would doze off I would slip away for an hour or two and clean up the kids and put them to bed. Sometimes I'd let them come to the hospital with me. But most nights I'd put them to sleep and lock the doors and windows. I never liked leaving them in that house all alone. But I had to.

"I would work from 11 o'clock at night until seven o'clock in the morning. Then I'd rush home and get the kids ready for school. Jeff was the youngest and from the age of three I had the local nuns look after him. I didn't like doing that, and in winter when it was cold and miserable, I really felt sorry for him. He was so small, so tiny.

"Once all the kids were taken care of I'd go back to the hospital and stay with Paul until school was finished. Then I'd pick them up, take them home, make their dinner, then go back to the hospital and on to work. In my lunch hour I used to run home to check on them and then run back to work."

Mary and Paul Fenech were used to running. When they were children they grew sensitive to the sounds of Stukas and Spitfires above what had once been an idyllic island home in the Mediterranean.

Invasion was as much a part of Malta's heritage as convicts and gold rushes were to Australia's. Ever since the Phonecians came in 1000 BC, the people from the tiny island off the Sicilian coast had grown accustomed to strangers on their sun-kissed shores. The Apostle Paul had converted the Maltese to Christianity after being shipwrecked there and re-marked on the hospitality of his rescuers.

Over the last 3000 years the Maltese had been ruled by the Greeks, the Carthaginians, Romans, Arabs, Sicilians, the Vatican, the Turks, the French under Napoleon, and finally the British. The island's location, amid the vital sea routes between Italy and Africa, gave the rulers of Malta strategic naval strength. In the Second World War, the British Government made the Maltese human targets by establishing great naval bases to guard the important sea lanes.

The cliffs and caves on the island's rocky coast protected submarines and the ancient Roman catacombs became bomb shelters for the sick, the frightened and the hungry.

"My mother and father had 14 children," Mary Fenech recalls, her sad eyes staring through thick glasses but still showing the sharp edge of misery cutting deep into her reserves of emotion. "Eight of them died during the fighting. Our whole village was destroyed. Three houses we lived in were all blown apart. I can remember coming out of church one Sunday and as I left the bombs came and killed almost everyone inside. I found my father's sandals buried among the stones. But somehow he was still alive."

Paul Fenech blamed the dank, damp ruins where he hid from the war outside, for the poor health that made him an invalid.

"There was bombing day in and day out. If you took all the bombs the Germans dropped on us in the war, their combined weight, would sink the island right under the sea. There wouldn't have been one house that wasn't damaged by fighting.

"There were bomb shelters built from the catacombs, but a lot of the time when I was a kid I had no brains. I used to run through the ruins when I'd hear the Stukas and the Spitfires fighting it out. I remember running along and hearing people screaming underneath me. It was like earthquakes every day. There were trapped bodies under great masses of stone. There was no way you could get them out. You just had to let them lie there and scream until they died. The sound of the cannons and the pom poms kept us awake all night, every night.

"I remember people lying on top of each other, in the catacombs, huddled together, and the sounds of dripping water, the poms poms, the bombing and the screams."

King George VI awarded the people of Malta a collective George Cross in 1942 for their bravery under fire. It was the highest possible civilian honour in the British Commonwealth but small consolation to the dead and the maimed, the blind and the sick.

Mary Fenech never learnt to read or write, not even in the language of her people. She spent her school days dodging bullets and bombs and seeing her homes levelled by enemies who often looked no more menacing than tiny sparrows in the blue skies above. Forty years after the war Mary needs her family and friends to read to her the newspaper accounts of her youngest son's exploits so she can paste them in her carefully collated scrapbook.

Paul Fenech, who learnt reluctantly to steal and trick his way out of hunger during the war, became a cinema operator when the hostilities ceased. He was self-motivated with the same kind of tremendous drive and will to succeed that would make his son stand out during his very first boxing lesson.

"I left school in Malta early because of the war", he would say. "I had to be cunning to keep my family alive. There were two girls and four boys in our family and I was the eldest boy. It was my job to find food and bring it home. My father earnt good money as a foreman at the dockyards, bringing home something like six pounds a week. But during the war it didn't matter how much money you had because it was impossible to buy anything. You had to pinch it.

"I went around the stores with my best clothes on, looking like a boy from the upper classes. Then a shirt would go into the pillow slip and a bag of sugar under the shoulder. In those days you stole to live. Jeff used to make me so angry when I'd find out he'd stolen things. He never needed to pinch anything."

Paul's job as a projectionist took him throughout Malta where he quickly earnt a reputation as an ambitious and industrious young man. He worked the Radio City Opera House, the West End Theatre, the Tivoli, the Coliseum in Valetta, the Carlton.

"But the standard of life in Malta changed little after the war. The British had promised us the world if they won, but they seemed to forget about us once the fighting stopped. My father was in El Alamein and he wanted me to go there. But my application to come to Australia came through and I thought it would be better if I went to a new country, one that didn't have so much trouble and heartache.

"I remember thinking that it was all bush and tin sheds and kangaroos. I brought thick blankets with me to use as mattresses because I thought I would have to sleep under the stars. I had hoped to get a job in the cinema here, but that involved going to tech and all that, so I finished up taking a job as a storeman."

Paul arrived in Sydney having just turned 19, and ahead of him was a brave new world with everything in store for a man who wanted to work hard. He lived in a cramped room in inner-city Redfern.

While still in his teens he was smitten with the thrill of boxing. But as he grew older and more pragmatic, and even despite the subsequent success of his youngest child in the international arena, Paul would come to regard it as "nothing more than two grown men belting into each other".

"But in my young days I loved the boxing. I even tried it myself. But I could never go the full round. Later I realised my ticker was crook all along."

Paul met his wife in 1952, three months after she arrived from Malta. "Her father had worked for the army back home and he was very strict," he recalled. "He wouldn't let us go anywhere together unless someone like a bodyguard went along too. So Mary and I decided to get married."

Children came every couple of years — Rita, believe it or not, the best fighter in the family, then Godfrey, a brooding local hero his younger brothers idiolised, Eric and Henry, who were constantly fighting baby brother Jeff, and Veronica, who was Jeff's confidant and closest friend, and was to be his most vocal supporter in the Los Angeles Olympic arena.

Jeffrey Fenech was born on May 28, 1964, 12 hours after his cousin Richard. "Jeff would have been called Richard," says Mary, "But he was born at seven in the night and my sister-in-law had her baby at seven in the morning and had called her boy Richard. I loved that name because my favourite TV show was Richard the Lionheart. My sister-in-law beat me to it by 12 hours."

It was a gravely sick Paul Fenech who first laid eyes on his sixth child. He'd gone to work every day until the night he "died" and was jolted back to life.

"In those days doctors didn't know much about heart trouble," Paul said shortly before his death. "They thought I had pleurisy. My first operation was a valvotomy where the doctors opened up the valve in the heart. It was unsuccessful. And so was the next one."

There were many other operations and heart attacks too. Paul suffered blood poisoning, gout and once even ballooned up to 20 stone, double his normal weight, because of a build-up in body fluids.

"My dad was always sick," Jeff explains. "Just before the return fight with Shingaki he was in intensive care. The doctor called us all in and told us he was going to die. He made us shave him and clean him up. I cried all the time I was there and never let go of his hand. He whispered to me that he'd be at my next fight. And he was."

Shortly before he defended his WBC super-bantamweight title against Greg Richardson, Fenech was rushed from a training session to visit his father's hospital bedside.

"One day my dad would look a million dollars and the next he'd have blood pouring from his mouth and would go white as a ghost," Fenech says. "When I went into see him at the hospital he was so sick the doctors couldn't even operate.

"Dad whispered to me that he was sorry he had been so sick and that if he had been healthy he could've done so much more for me. I told him not to be so stupid. That I loved him so much.

"He was always a stubborn bludger. He'd be dying and wouldn't let anyone help him."

Mary interrupts with her version of another near miss before the sad finale when there would be no comeback.

"Paul was coughing up so much blood that time. It wasn't his heart but he was taking so many drugs for his sickness that his insides were soft, like tissues. He had a terrible cold and by coughing all the time he burst inside. He was coughing up buckets of blood and choking on it. And all the time he was screaming 'bye bye, bye bye'. Bleeding to death and he wouldn't let me call the ambulance." ■

4
The Lie

*"We learn to put up with pain, push pain
aside, disregard it entirely. We know how it is
to carry on in the face of pain"*
lightheavyweight champ
Tommy Loughran, 1928.

As a baby Jeff Fenech would often be taken to visit his father in hospital and sometimes to the factories his mother had to clean. He grew up to the smells of disinfectant and cleaning fluid.

"He was a quiet little boy," his mother remembers, "I could leave him on the floor for hours playing with books, drawings, cards, toy horses, toy soldiers."

From the time he could walk the future champion was competitive. His mother liked to dress him in suits and shoes and ties that most of the time cost more than the meagre budget would allow. But beneath the cute smile and the wide-eyed innocence of childhood was a budding hoodlum. A kid who even at five or six told everyone he wanted to be the best. That second best would never be good enough.

"He was always obsessed with fitness and winning," Paul once recollected. "I can remember Jeff crying his eyes out one day because his football team had been beaten. He kept saying over and over again, 'It's all their stupid fault. They wouldn't listen to me, they wouldn't listen.' He was five years old.

"Even back then he had to be the boss of everyone. Jeff was always a bright boy, and even though he never liked school, I always hoped he would get a good job. Maybe work in a bank or something like that."

But as a boy, the only thing the youngest Fenech knew about banks, was that people robbed them.

With his parents away most of the time and with plenty of

Aboriginal kids in St Peters to fight in childhood race riots, Fenech was already starting to enjoy the feeling of his knuckles hitting someone in the mouth. Or his little hands knotted tightly around another boy's throat.

The word 'wog' was the signal for attack, just like the sight of another kid with pocket money in his pants. He learnt how to cheat at cards, how to wait for other kids to get drunk or stoned before cleaning up with a hidden ace, he found out the homes where there was milk money waiting to be pinched and discovered that if a paper boy wasted enough time searching for change, he could get to keep it.

"I had such a strict upbringing that I swore my kids would have it easier," Mary Fenech admits. "I was under the key so much I had to let my kids have their freedom. I was never allowed to go anywhere and I wanted my children to enjoy themselves. I let Jeff go anywhere he wanted."

The baby of the Fenech family made the most of his freedom. "When I was seven or eight a kid at school hit me in the face with a shovel. One of those little toy plastic shovels," he said. "It didn't break any bones or anything, but whenever I wanted to stay home from school I just had to touch my nose and the blood would pour out everywhere. I stayed home all the time.

"I used to be an altar boy, but that never stopped me from doing anything. When I was a kid I used to tell Mum I was going to the pictures. But we'd all meet, 30 or 40 of us, and go to the Showground speedway looking for fights. If you climbed the wall, you could get in through the ladies' toilets. A whole big gang of us used to go through there all at once and the ladies in the toilet would be screaming and yelling. Other times we'd go up to the golf course hill and wait to start fights with other kids walking home. The weapons were knives, baseball bats and those kung-fu sticks. Mum would always ask me what happened and I'd always tell her that some kid picked on me, called me a wog, and that I had to fight him. If I ever got into trouble, I'd always tell Mum, never Dad. He had a terrible temper. He'd get his belt off and really whip us. Sometimes I'd duck and dodge or hide under the blankets with my brother Henry. But it still always hurt."

Paul Fenech remembered the days when his son was an enemy of the law and he would laugh at life's ironies.

"You know I thought my children were all little angels" he'd say, "I never suspected Jeff was fighting and stealing.

Then one day I was having a drink at the Town and Country Hotel in St. Peters and I overheard this fellow talking.

"'Watch out for those Fenech boys,' he was telling his friend, 'they're bad news, real trouble.' I couldn't believe my ears, that they were talking about my kids. But Jeff would never tell me anything. If he ever admitted to something he usually lied about it."

Living on the streets gave Jeff Fenech a rare cunning. He boasts that he can outsmart anyone, no matter their education or background. That he can tell anyone a lie and make them believe him.

"When the police would come to my house or when my Dad would start asking me questions about things I did, I'd just look them right in the eye and lie about it. If they didn't believe me I'd just go red in the face and scream and scream and I'd start to cry until I convinced them I was telling the truth. I'd talk so fast that their brains couldn't keep up with me.

"I suppose I was always the ring-leader. I was a self-taught thief. They'd be all my own ideas, whether it was pinching money at the markets or changing price labels in a shop. I wanted the best of everything but I wanted everything without paying for it. But mostly I got into trouble because I was bored. A lot of parents in the neighbourhood wouldn't let their kids play football with me because I was always bashing them up."

In his boxing career Fenech's deception came in handy.

"We fighters understand lies," the eloquent light-heavyweight, Jose Torres once said, "What's a feint? What's a left hook off the jab? What's an opening? What's thinking one thing and doing another?"

Torres' friend, the even more eloquent American writer Norman Mailer, had similar thoughts, while observing the preparations for the cataclysmic battle between Muhammad Ali and George Foreman in the steaming heart of Africa.

All boxers were liars, Mailer reasoned, great boxers were simply great liars.

They lied every time they said they could win when they knew they would lose. They lied every time they were screaming for mercy but gritted their teeth with hate.

Boxers use the most brutal form of chicanery to win fights.

"One of the primary things boxing is about is lying," Joyce Carol Oates claims. "It's about systematically cultivating a double personality; the self in society, the self in the ring."

Early in Fenech's amateur days he learnt how to aim for
the body but shoot to the head. He studied techniques to show
the left but throw the right. He set well-concealed traps for
his victims, he disguised vulnerability while masking pain
and fatigue.

When he was a kid Fenech lied so much that fooling opponents in later life was like taking candy from a baby.

When Constable Pat Jarvis, international rugby league forward and a police officer stationed at nearby Newtown, first
met Fenech, he would remember the speed of the young
tough's mouth.

"I remember seeing Jeff brandishing a cricket bat outside a
house where he had a family trapped inside," Jarvis recalls.
"It was a domestic problem. The people in the house had their
side to the story and Jeff had his. But Jeff was jumping up and
down, dropping the name of his trainer Johnny Lewis every
now and then to try to get out of it. I remember saying to the
officer with me that the kid had a big mouth and it would get
him into a lot of trouble."

There is a misconception in the story of Fenech's rapid rise
to boxing stardom that Jarvis discovered the aggressive street
fighter and directed him to Lewis' gym so the ferocity could be
channelled into more lawful areas. The story is false. Fenech
was already taking boxing lessons from Lewis when he first
met Jarvis, although the myth of the policeman's involvement
was infinitely more cinematic.

Boxing, however, became a means for Fenech to release the
anger that welled in him. He could hit other people legally,
maybe one day even get paid for it, and he could wash away
his anger in another boy's tears.

He made sacrifices in time and effort, but then so has everyone around him.

"I used to put my pension cheques aside so he could go to
tournaments," Mary says, "And I helped Jeff raffle gifts he
got from stores that donated things to him. We would go
through the streets of St Peters selling the tickets and making
money where we could."

Paul and Mary didn't enjoy seeing their son in a sport
where the prime objective was to hurt your opponent before
he hurt you. But Mary travelled everywhere her son fought in
Australia. A tiny, bespectacled figure leading the cheers for
her boy. If she had the money she would have flown by his
side to overseas tournaments, too. She didn't like boxing, but

she felt reassured that her son was safe if she could hold his hand before a fight.

"I never missed one of Jeff's fights in Australia. I was always so scared he would get hurt. Johnny told me Jeff was a very good fighter and he would always make sure that nothing bad ever happened to my boy. But every time he fought I was on the end of my chair."

Fenech's father would temper his pride with reality.

"What's the good of all the money in the world if you end up with brain damage?" he would ask with a similar argument doctors had been putting forward for 100 years.

"I don't want my son fighting for too long. I wanted him to stop, but he is his own boss. The best thing I ever saw in my whole life was the crowd at the first Shingaki fight. It wasn't just that he won the title. But it was there that I first realised my son was a hero. Thousands of people were there and they'd paid good money to see my son fight another man for the world championship. But, of course, all the time I was worried. Against Coffee there was one big punch right at the end that caught Jeff flush on the chin. I nearly collapsed."

The Fenech children grew up in Paul's weatherboard cottage in St Peters. There were good times and bad. One of the worst came in a living room neatly stacked with trophies and photographs, momentoes of a young man's achievements in the cruellest sport of all.

"Seeing Jeffrey fight at the Olympic Games was fantastic, and shattering too," Paul remembered. "When he started boxing I liked the fact he was making a name for himself but I didn't want to encourage his boxing. So all along I kept quiet. But I watched every fight from the Olympics, round by round. Mary and I stayed up all night and morning watching him. Jeff would phone us from Los Angeles to tell us what time he was fighting and we would sit up for hours waiting with our fingers crossed before his fight came on. After he fought the Yugoslav boy, Redzepovski, I could see the look in Jeff's eyes, I felt the same way. All that hard work he put in for nothing.

"Who knows? Maybe that loss at the Olympics was the best thing that ever happened to my son. Without that little Yugoslav boy, Jeff wouldn't be where he is today." ■

5
The Hood

"Rocky Graziano didn't box, he threw cobblestones. If permitted he would cheerfully have used a knife or blackjack or grenade"
Red Smith, US writer.

Until he met Johnny Lewis, Jeff Fenech didn't really care what other people thought of him. He mightn't have had the respect of society and its minders, but he had the respect of just about every tough on the streets of Marrickville, Newtown, Erskineville and St Peters.

Those days weren't too bad as long as you didn't get caught. For Fenech the old brushes with authority had their moments. He knew he was smart and cunning and very plausible, which all came in handy on the rare occasions he was nabbed. Throughout his long dalliance with petty crime he believed that was the real motivation, the thrill of the chase or the chance to outsmart everyone else, whether it was his parents, his teachers, the cops or any of the hoodlum gangs he tangled with so often.

He remembered walking with his mother to St Pius at Enmore for his first day of school. "I suppose I didn't really walk," he recalled. "She had to drag me. I was kicking and screaming and crying. I knew I'd hate it."

He hated losing his first fight, too, to the kid wielding a plastic spade that sent the future world champion home to his mother with a nose bleed and a determination that it would not happen again. It did, of course, because in gang warfare there are no prisoners — only winners and casualties.

Fenech might have turned into the sweet little boy in fancy European clothing his mother always wanted him to be had it not been for his father's grave health problems. As a boy he had no guidance except for the time he would spend at the home of his football coach Ralph Speechley. To the kids of

Marrickville, Ralph's home was a sanctuary. Ralph fought a losing battle.

"Unless someone has been through this sort of thing they wouldn't understand," Fenech says, "My Mum spent all her time visiting hospitals, working and trying to take care of us.

"Often she would fall asleep as she sat by my father's bed at the hospital. Although Dad had been very sick before I was born, my first memory of him was when he gave me a belting for getting up to mischief. All us kids were petrified of him. He had a terrible temper and if he found out any of us had been causing trouble, it always meant the belt. Perhaps it was because I was the youngest, but most of the time I could lie my way out of it. But I remember one time when my lying didn't save me. We had been accused of pinching money from a taxi and of course we denied it. The driver came to the house and complained to Dad but I jumped up and down and screamed and cried until he believed me. Later I was telling my brother Henry where I'd hidden the money and Dad was listening at the door. Off came the belt and we ducked under the blankets for protection, crying our eyes out."

Fenech can't remember a day at school when he didn't get the strap or the cane. "I was always in trouble. If it wasn't the strap, then I was kept in. One day I was locked in the art room and they forgot about me. But I broke a window and started throwing paint onto the woman's lawn next door. They finally came to let me out at 8 o'clock."

He might have been bright enough to pass any school exam, but he preferred to cheat. If he earnt good marks by studying it would only prove he was smarter than his classmates. But if he cheated and got away with it, he felt he was proving himself smarter than the teachers, by putting it over them as well.

Without a hint of remorse, Fenech reflects on his school days: "I was always in the top classes because I cheated and got great marks. They put me in with the square heads and I'd sleep through most of the classes. Every test, I cheated."

He would go into an exam with solutions to problems scribbled on the inside of a tie or on his leg under his shorts. Once he broke into the staff room at lunch time and swiped the answer to an exam that was coming up that afternoon. But mostly he positioned himself in the examination room alongside the brighter kids and stood over them for full co-operation. "I had a bad reputation and I also had brothers who were well-known for being tough. That sort of thing can make life easy at school. Sometimes I wouldn't even have to fight. I'd just give some kid a biff and make him buy me lunch. I was a little altar boy. I was spoiled. I was the baby. Mum and dad had no idea I was a real little thug. I am sorry now that I did a lot of those things, but I got a kick out of it at the time. In fact, they were the only kicks I knew."

While Paul and Mary Fenech looked on their youngest offspring as an angelic child, he was plunging headlong toward a life behind bars. "When Dad was in hospital and Mum was working or visiting him I'd always get into trouble," says Fenech.

"Of course, they didn't know what we were getting up to."

Fenech still vividly remembers the carnage of those days of gang warfare. The Newtown Hoods, as his gang was known, had their losses as well as victims. Bloody kids lying unconscious on the streets, in darkened parks and unattended railway carriages with their girlfriends crying over them. "After one fight I remember the police cars driving onto Moore Park Golf Course and one of my brothers grabbing me and dragging me away . . . and running all the way to St Peters. I remember hiding under a car and lifting myself up under the exhaust and the cops flashing torches all around me."

But Fenech wasn't always so lucky. Like the time in Hyde Park in the city when a member of a rival gang smashed him across the jaw with the plaster cast on his right arm. The Marrickville Mauler couldn't open his mouth for days. Inevitably the law closed in. After a sickening brawl at Central Station, the railway police swooped and he was up on four charges of assault. The newspapers played it up big. A 10-year-old boy was knocked out cold by a garbage can. His older brother had retaliated by stabbing his attacker through the lung.

As Fenech recalls it, the stabbing victim died, but was revived by a nurse who happened to be walking past. After the railway brawl Fenech and his brother Henry were locked up at the Yasmar Shelter in Ashfield. He was not quite 12 at the time. When the matter finally came before the court the two brothers were sentenced to three and a half months to three years, what was known as a general term.

"Mum was screaming as they took me out of the court and locked me in a little cell," Fenech recalled. "I can remember when they took us in the paddy-wagon. Henry, who was 16 at the time, went to Mt Penang near Gosford and I was taken to Ormond, a place in Thornleigh. We were both crying, but it didn't stop us spitting at cars from the paddy-wagon and sticking up our fingers at them, pretending we were real bad crims. Real gangsters.

"They dropped me off first and I was real scared. I got into trouble straight away. They cut off my hair and blokes started laughing. I got into a fight and the guards made me scrub concrete with a toothbrush." But as always, Fenech quickly wised up. He befriended all the guards by appealing to their liking for sport. He was made captain of the centre's football team.

"But I still wanted desperately to get out. On a Sunday you'd always be looking to see if your parents were coming through the gate. My Mum would have to get up at 5 o'clock in the morning, because after she would visit me, she would go on to Gosford to see Henry. Now that I'm so much older and wiser I'm really ashamed of what we did to her."

Fenech spent two months at the boys home. He impressed the guards so much that they let him live in the Privileges Cottage. He made toast for the officers and ate extra helpings as a reward for good behaviour. Every weekend his mother came to visit and every weekend she would cry.

When they let Fenech out, he never went back. Although for the next five years he defied the law to catch him. Anything for a chase.

While Jeff and Henry were defying and tangling with the law, their eldest brother Godfrey always seemed to be a model citizen. "Eric and Godfrey never got into trouble," Jeff recalls. "Godfrey would always be there to try to smooth things over when we had done the wrong thing."

Ironically, in 1987, when Jeff Fenech was a national hero and the first Australian to have held world boxing titles in two divisions, Godfrey was sentenced to life imprisonment for murder. ■

6
The Second Father

"Cus D'Amato raised Mike Tyson in every possible sense. He taught him about life. The boxing lessons were merely an additional tributary"
                              Jimmy Jacobs,
                    Tyson's co-manager, 1987.

When the trains roar along Sydney's western railway line every other minute, the tremors reach the Newtown Police Youth Club, shaking the doors and windows and drowning out some of the screams and laughter from dozens of grubby-faced kids inside.

It's been that way ever since they built the place.

The trains used to roar by the club when John Lewis was a boy, learning how to box 30 years ago. And it was like that when this suburban sanctuary for kids was a menacing eyesore, stained by sweat and pollution.

That was what the club was like in 1981 when Lewis arrived one afternoon to conduct his daily boxing classes and first clamped eyes on the street kid whose toughness was to change both their lives.

To Lewis and Fenech that day is as lasting and alluring as the smell of leather boxing gloves fresh from the factory.

"Back then I was training Jeff Malcolm for what we hoped would be a world title fight and I was also working with an amateur kid named Mark Cribb," Lewis recalls.

"I remember walking into the gym to train Mark, and there was this real tough-looking Turkish bloke waiting, and with him was a dark little fella who could have been Aboriginal or Italian. That was Jeff Fenech. They were both just sitting there watching the kids train and Jeff had overheard me telling Mark that he needed some good sparring."

They were the words that were to give Australia a real-life Rocky. The eavesdropping kid with the tough-looking Turk didn't have a clue about boxing. If he'd been asked to name three famous fighters, he'd have been stuck after Muhammad Ali. But he was more interested in making his own history.

"All of a sudden Jeff leapt up and said, 'I'll spar with him'," Lewis said. Jeff first came to the gym because he had nothing better to do, not because, as the popular story went, Pat Jarvis picked him up one day and steered him from a life of crime. Jeff intended to try out in the weights room, but heard a noise from the boxing gym. He went to investigate and liked what he saw. He wanted to spar right away.

Lewis wasn't sure what to make of the brash newcomer whose attitude mocked the hundreds of hours the trainer and his fighters spent working out.

Sure, he looked tough enough. His nose had more than its share of bumps and twists, and even then, Fenech had the build of a boxer. Several months working as a bricklayer and regular football training had developed a powerful back and shoulders, even for a 17-year-old not much over seven stone.

He had long, sinewy arms and strong, slim legs. The Turkish-looking boy with him looked like he'd kill for a hamburger.

But in Lewis' gym, rules were rules.

"That's not the way we do things here," Lewis told the cocky upstart. "Have you ever done any boxing before?"

"Nuh. But I'll be all right," the kid replied.

"If you're so keen to be a fighter, how about coming up here tomorrow and doing some training?" Lewis suggested.

"If I come up tomorrow, can I spar 'im then?"

"Yeah, but be here by four o'clock."

Fenech was in for the shock of his life the next day. That was what Lewis thought. And with most things in boxing, he was right.

"The next day I got to the gym at three o'clock and there was Jeff sitting out the front waiting for me," Lewis recalls. "I didn't know if he was arrogant or shy, but in those days he didn't talk much. He'd cut his answers to a minimum. 'Yep' or 'Nuh'. That's about all you'd ever get out of him. Anyway, he got into the ring and I told Mark to take it easy. If Mark had gone flat out he'd have probably bashed the kid inside one round. But I told him to get some work out of the cheeky little bugger. Mark looked after him while they sparred, never going too hard or trying to hurt him. Jeff was raw, but he impressed me. It was obvious he was really stuffed, but he kept

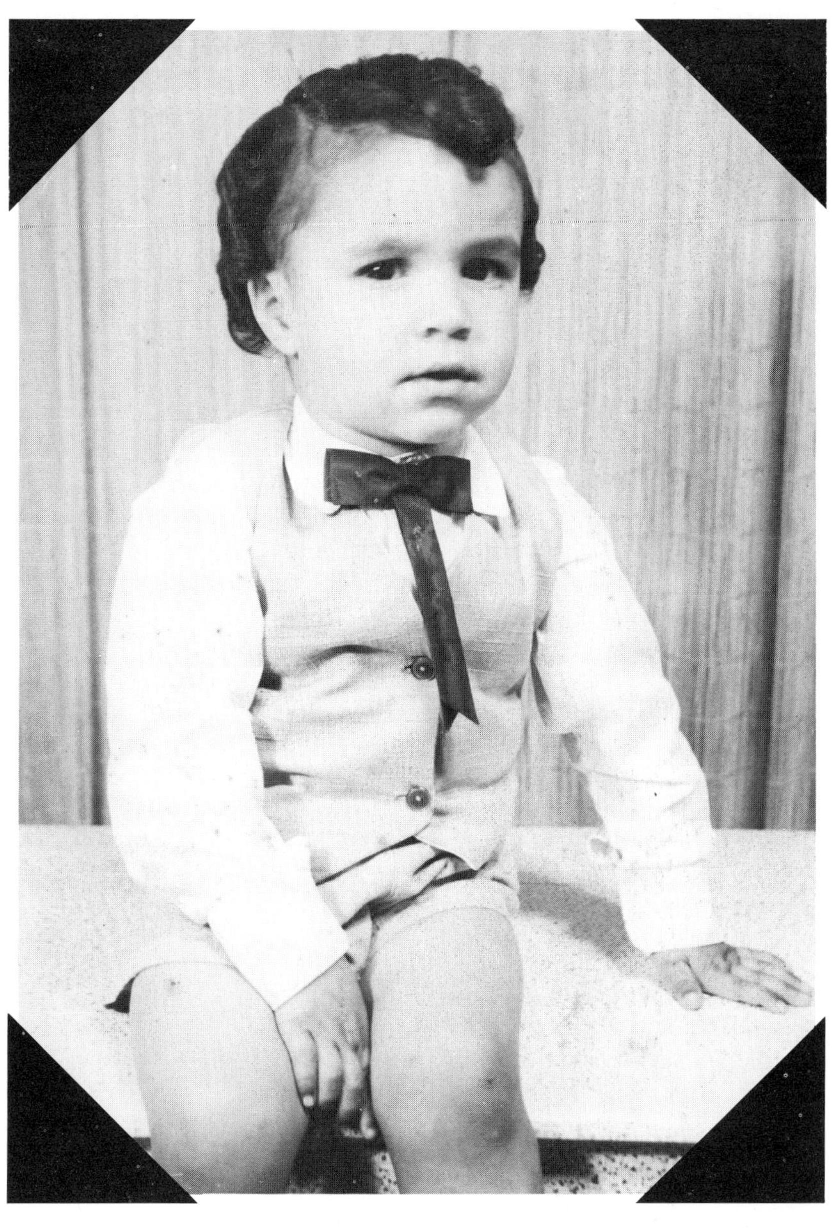

Fenech at the age of two. His mother liked dressing her baby in fancy clothes.

Above: Fenech loved the role of the gangster. Here he poses in fancy dress with South Sydney rugby league captain Mario Fenech (left) and friend Joe Aquilina.

Above left: By the age of five, Fenech had fallen in love with rugby league, and, *above right,* at 14, and with a stint in a boys' home behind him, he was dreaming of playing hooker for the Australian team.

In Fiji for an amateur tournament that landed them all in trouble, Fenech still had a great time with trainer John Lewis and Peter Mitrevski (left).

Above: Fenech as an amateur. He was all aggression against Samoan Lautapo Ofa Wong King but (below) his anger couldn't beat the skills of Heo Yung Mo in their second fight in Bangkok.

going. I'd ask him if he was okay and he'd just say 'yep' and keep fighting."

After the workout had finished, Fenech was hurting, but unbowed, and Lewis suggested he should become a regular at the gymnasium. That maybe in 12 months or so he'd be ready for a real fight, in a real boxing ring and with real trophies. That he shouldn't really spar someone like Mark Cribb until he'd learned some of boxing's basics.

"I'm right. I'll spar 'im again tomorrow," Fenech retorted.

Lewis took a keener interest.

"The next night I wanted to see if Jeff was just a big mouth with nothing to back it up," Lewis says, "In the second round of their spar I got Mark to start ripping some punches underneath. When he started belting him in the belly, Jeff started to slow down, started to shorten stride. But even though he was being hurt and outclassed, he still wouldn't give up. I was impressed. He must have been hurt, but he wouldn't show it. He'd just grit his teeth and start throwing punches back. He was certainly game. The next day Jeff started training with me and I can't remember him ever missing a day since."

Lewis hadn't missed too many days in the gym either. Not since he started boxing at the same Police Boys Club in 1957. He was 13, a shade over five stone and sparking a love affair with a sport that has made him both a father figure and coach to so many young hopefuls.

Since meeting Fenech, much of Lewis' hair has fallen out, and what's left, has gone grey. He is now 44 years old and has lived in Erskineville for almost all of them. Six years after that first meeting Lewis still mispronounces the fighter's name. Fe-NECK instead of FEN-eck.

He likes eating spaghetti in cheap Italian restaurants and he enjoys the occasional beer with his regular mates. Like his father, he is a joker and prankster. Fun to be with. He can impersonate just about everyone, from the neighbourhood drunk to any number of the "fleas" which infest the sport of boxing like it was a mangy dog.

He speaks in a quiet nasal tone that is straight out of a '40s boxing movie where the trainers are all called "Whitey" and where the managers smoke big cigars and steal their fighters' money.

He has been known to make Fenech cry with laughter, but is so publicity shy that he almost always looks grim in newspaper photographs and television interviews.

Lewis loves Erskineville and the boxing gym where he started punching the bags 30 years ago. He's proud that he can walk down "Erko Road" and not meet a "bad friend", that he played rugby league and Australian rules football and was never reported, never sent off.

He's worked as a Sydney County Council signwriter for 28 years and despite the financial rewards of being trainer to a world boxing champion Lewis has always considered his role in boxing as a hobby, albeit, a hobby that cuts deep into his time and emotions.

"I never really wanted to make money out of boxing," he insists. "I've worked at the same job since I was 16 and I've always felt it proper to go out each day and work for a living.

"The biggest kick I can ever get out of boxing is to see a kid working in the gym for months, day in and day out, to put his faith and trust in me, and then go out and win a fight without getting hit. No amount of money could ever be better than to have a little bloke come up to you after a fight and put his arms around you and say 'thanks Johnny'. You get a real big kick out of seeing someone you've trained years later and finding out that life was good to them. That they didn't have to do the wrong thing by people to get by.

"A lot of the kids I've trained have been headed for jail, but a lot of them got off that road through the fight game. I love Jeff Fenech, but to me he's no more important than a 12-year-old getting ready for his first fight. There's at least a dozen kids training at the gym, who are just as important to me as Jeff. He might be the hero and he might be in the papers every day, but that really doesn't affect my way of thinking. If Jeff retired tomorrow I'd still be up at the Police Boys at 4 o'clock the next afternoon. You know, there's a lot of things crook with the fight game. There always has been and there probably always will be.

"In Sydney there's a lot of jealous bastards. There are people who make boxing a rotten sport. Since Jeff won the world title I've been more disappointed with some people than at any time in my whole life. Jealousy is like a cancer, except cancer gets you quicker. I let my emotions get carried away at the Shingaki and Coffee fights because there were so many blokes I knew who were just hoping Jeff would get bashed. Rather than see someone kick on, they'd rather drag you down into the hole with them.

"The thing I've always liked most about boxing is the

fighter. There aren't too many who are a low breed. I take my hat off to any kid with the gumption to get in and have a go. There's a lot of blokes who'd king-hit someone in a pub, but wouldn't have the guts to fight someone in a boxing ring."

In a sport with a repution for producing more shysters than saints, Fenech found a man of genuine virtue when he walked into the Newtown gym.

He wasn't really looking for anyone. He was just a bored young man looking for something to do. He found Lewis who first went to that big old building when it was a big new building and has been a familiar face there ever since.

"I started boxing when Jack Blom and Snowy McFadyen were the trainers there," Lewis recalls. "I just wandered in to the club one day and everything just happened from there. In those days we had some great boxers training at Newtown. Blokes like Billy and Danny Males, Freddie Casey and Jackie Bruce. Jack Blom was a real dapper bloke who could shine a shoe like no one else. And he was always taking the Erko kids on trips. He'd not only take the good fighters away to tournaments, but he'd always make sure the kids were part of the team. Just about every week we'd go to Sydney Stadium or to places like Canberra or Young or Griffith. It was great for us city kids to get out in the fresh air. Jack never liked anyone feeling left out."

Thirty years later, Lewis' Newtown Police Youth Club boxing team would be as fiercely close-knit as ever, the world champion even taking time out from advanced training to watch his young gym-mates having their first fights in amateur singlets.

"After 18 months, Jack and Snowy left the gym and Dick O'Connor took over. Dick was probably the greatest trainer I've ever been associated with. I believe he'd been a pretty good fighter in his own right, but had been barred from the ring because of a bad eye. I thought I could have done very well as a boxer under his care. I never lost a fight with Dick in my corner. He trained some real good boxers like David Floyd. There wasn't another fight trainer in the country who could get near Dick O'Connor — in fact he was so well regarded that a lot of top fighters who were working with other trainers would come down to the Police Boys' to go through punches with him. He'd shut down the gymnasium and then work with them behind closed doors. He could have big-noted himself, but he'd always keep it a secret. That was the kind of bloke he was.

"I think my greatest asset as a boxing trainer is that I genuinely care for the blokes I train, inside the ring and out. Dick really loved his fighters too. When I was 17, some illness cropped up in his family and he left the gym. He told me he'd be back in four weeks, but I haven't seen him to this day. Since I was the oldest kid, they made me the trainer and that's how my career as a boxing coach really started."

For the last 27 years, Lewis has been teaching people to fight. He's seen gutsy kids come and go, hard-hitters shine and fade, brilliant boxers who weren't brilliant enough. In Jeff Fenech he saw something special — speed, power, courage, intensity, desire. So many necessities that a top-class fighter spends years developing. And yet here was a little kid who had them all.

He may not have been able to beat Mark Cribb when he first walked into the gym, but Fenech was willing to learn. And Lewis was a great teacher.

Like Fenech says "he is a quiet, unassuming man who commands tremendous respect because he gives people tremendous respect".

The first boxer Lewis ever trained was Alan "Bull" Parker. "Bull was only about nine then, and he fought at Hornsby the same night I had my last amateur bout. Bull would be about 34 now. He still trains at the Police Boys most days. Along with Pat Penning, he's one of my oldest friends and he played a big role in helping Jeff reach the top. In my early days of training, I had a fair bit of success with Martin and Kevin Ross. Martin beat a lot of great fighters like Rocky Mattioli and Charkey Ramon in the amateurs and he was the first bloke I had who turned professional."

Over the years Lewis developed a close association with some of the biggest names in boxing. But always he tried to keep a low profile.

He was one of the few to farewell Lionel Rose on his way to Japan and a world title win over Fighting Harada. He worked corners for years, never stealing the limelight from anyone, all the time building up a knowledge of boxing second to none and a sense of humanity and fair play that no amount of teaching can produce.

Since 1981, Lewis has been a father confessor, best friend and helping hand to Fenech and to many others whose names were more small print than headlines.

Always he believed boxing was a sport going nowhere. That it was a hobby and a means of salvation for some, but that it offered no career except for the few, the very few, who could capture the public imagination and fight like a hive of crazed hornets.

In Fenech, Lewis found a kid who could go all the way.

"I watched him for a few days and I thought 'God strewth, this kid could be anything'. You only had to show him something once and he could do it. He was so strong for his size and he had this incredible will to be the best. It was that tremendous drive that separated him from other fighters. You could see it in his eyes. You could see it in the way he punched the bags or chased after a bloke in the ring. He just wouldn't settle for being ordinary. He had to be number one. If a kid hit him, he'd hit back three times, four times. He'd never let anyone gain the upper hand. Yet he was always sick. He still is. He's always got a cold or an earache or sore feet, but he never shirks it in the gym or in the boxing ring. Even when he was a little kid, training for his first amateur fight, he was more professional than a lot of big names. With him, training is all or nothing. Depending on their abilities and progress I usually keep kids in the gym for six, 12 even 18 months before they have a fight. Jeff was in the gym just six weeks before his first tournament. He was a natural. Anybody could have told you he was going to be a great fighter. I still wanted to keep him in the gym, but he was always nagging me 'When can I fight, when can I fight?' So we went out to Blacktown and that was the start of great things for him.

"There's a great bond between us. Probably because I've had to do things for him that other people couldn't have done. We're a lot closer probably than any other trainer and fighter in the world. I've had to help him through personal problems and I know he's dropped my name to get out of trouble more than once when he was starting out. I think the bond has something to do with him wanting to always be the best. I worked very hard to get him to the top and he realises that. Even when he was just a novice he'd drag me along to watch him play football. Get me over to meet his family. He sort of adopted me as a second father. In the ring, Jeff puts complete trust in me. He never questions any of my decisions. He knows that even if he was a mile ahead on points in the 15th round and was badly hurt that I'd throw in the towel without hesitating for a second. He knows his health is more important to me than any amount of money.”

Lewis has always called the shots and wouldn’t have it any other way. He’s responsible for Fenech’s safety and in boxing a split second here or there can mean the difference between finishing your career with all your faculties or ending up with a lot of regrets. Lewis used to go to bat for Fenech in the early days when his fighter was in the wrong.

“He’d tell me things that he wouldn’t tell anyone else and in some ways I helped ease the burden. He had more problems than most kids and I was always someone he could talk to. A friend when he needed one, sort of a social worker I guess. We’ve come a long way together. Jeff’s still got a lot to learn and maybe luck has played the biggest part in his success. He’s certainly had more breaks go his way than most. But he’ll never stop trying to learn in the gym, and just like that first day against Mark Cribb, he’ll never say he’s tired.

“All along, I sensed something special in the kid. At first I thought he was a smart arse and a show-off and a lair. But I lost that feeling soon enough. Boxing really did save Jeff as a citizen. Who knows where he’d be if he hadn’t shown ability in the sport! All the counselling in the world doesn’t work for some people. For Jeff, boxing was better than counselling. He’s cunning and street-wise, but he’s not the most mature bloke in the world and I’ve had to put him straight and threaten to quit on him a few times. But he’s also fiercely loyal. He’ll stick by you when it matters most. He knows he does the wrong things at times. But if he disappoints you one day, he’ll try and make it up to you the next.” ■

7
Signs Of Greatness

*"Boxing is a great sport. Some people think
that it degrades the man who practises it. On
the contrary it elevates. It encourages a man, it
teaches him the discipline of life, and combat
creates respect for the rival who is worthy."*
Georges Carpentier, light-heavyweight
champion of the world, 1920.

Six weeks with the smell of perspiration and leather in the claustrophobic confines of the sweatbox that is the Newtown Police Boys' boxing gym, and Jeff Fenech was ready for his first official bout. As far as Lewis was concerned, it was an abnormally short preparation for one of his fighters, but Fenech had shown extraordinary aptitude. Pat Jarvis, who was also training at Newtown to galvanise his rugby league conditioning, had told the trainer that his star prodigy was something of a local public enemy, something that Lewis already suspected.

It wasn't long before Lewis was given a close-up inspection of the other side to Jeff Fenech, the budding amateur boxer. Twenty minutes after his first official contest, an amateur debut that was impressive, if perhaps a little uncontrolled, Fenech was showing the audience at the Blacktown Police Boys Club that he didn't need a referee or gloves to prove his mettle. He'd weighed just seven stone 11 pounds in outpointing another youngster named Craig Easey from the Fairfield Police Boys Club, but Lewis, although suitably impressed by Fenech's aggressive approach, was staggered more by his reaction to pressures outside the ring.

"We were walking out of the club after the tournament when all of a sudden Jeff went berserk, completely crazy. I didn't know what was going on. Suddenly, he'd grabbed this big bloke from the footpath, turned him upside down and was ramming his head into the concrete. The bloke had said something about Jeff's girlfriend, Tania, and I don't think he ever knew what hit him. It all happened so fast. In one way, I was disgusted but in another I was laughing inside. I told Jeff if he didn't stop bashing the bloke he could kiss goodbye our friendship and forget about training with me for good. As soon as I grabbed him, he let the big bloke go. That impressed me. Even then, he realised I was the boss and was prepared to go along with whatever I thought was best. I guess that's when we started to become close friends. Jeff knew I always wanted the best things to happen for him and that belting blokes on the road was a mug's caper, with no future. But all the while going home I remember saying to myself over and over: 'If he can fight half as good in the ring as he can on the road he could be anything'."

Fenech was willing to listen and learn from Lewis. He may have been a professor on the streets, but in the boxing gym, he was still in kindergarten, a brilliant pupil, but still unlearned. He was quickly starting to adapt his natural killer instinct though, bringing the murderous glare and the pathological hatred towards opponents to the stricter regulations of amateur boxing.

Sonny Liston had it much tougher than Jeff Fenech. Sonny grew up as one of 25 children to an Arkansas sharecropper who whipped his boy every day until the kid almost looked forward to the daily beatings. When he became the most feared heavyweight of his era, a monolith with a chilling stare and a killing pair of huge fists, Liston was interviewed by the American writer, Pete Hamill. The journalist tried for some human interest: "So I said: 'Sonny, how does it feel to see a man lying on the canvas with his eyes rolling in his head, his body twitching and his tongue hanging out?' He just looked down and matter-of-factly said: 'Makes me feel good'."

Fenech had shown that same killer instinct against the unknown Easey over three rounds of one-and-a-half minutes each. The fight took place on November 7, 1981, and the future champion of the world, fighting before just a few dozen parents and supporters in a youth club auditorium deep in Sydney's sprawling west, captured a one-sided decision after putting three standing counts on his opponent. Even in victory, he showed a recklessness Lewis would work hard to correct.

"Jeff won the fight easily but he was rushing far too much,"

Lewis recalls. "If he'd taken his time and worked off his jab, he'd probably have stopped the guy in a couple of rounds. But he was like a wild man, a caged lion, charging in like a miniature Jake LaMotta and throwing crazy punches from all angles."

With the win over Easey under his belt, Fenech was now salivating for more scalps in the sport he'd chosen over rugby league. If you took away the singlet and the gloves and the mouthguard he was now able to do what he loved even more than playing football. He could hit people and hurt them as much as he liked, over and over again, until someone rescued his victims. He could take out all his boredom and frustrations, all the latent violence that welled in him and gushed through to the surface whenever the bell sounded. His terror attacks on people who called him names or cut him off in the Marrickville traffic were becoming less and less frequent. He could still fight people, safe in the knowledge he would never be arrested wearing that learner's singlet and gloves.

The second fight in an already prosperous-looking career was scheduled for the RSL club in the beachside Sydney suburb of Bronte two weeks after his successful debut. It was also to provide the boxer with the first of many disappointments that lay ahead on the amateur trail. Yet Lewis believes what happened confirmed he and Fenech would become an inseparable team.

"The bloke Jeff was listed to fight was supposed to weigh around seven stone seven, but instead he got on the scales and went something like eight stone. There was no way I could let the fight go ahead and I told Jeff to pack his bag because we were going home. He was heartbroken, like a lost little boy. He'd really worked his guts out in the gym getting ready for the fight and he couldn't understand why I was letting a few pounds interfere with his plans. He really wanted to get in there and let out all the energy and adrenalin he'd built up. I told him that if he didn't want to do things my way there wasn't much use in him training with me.

"After he sat back a while I guess he realised that I only canned the fight because I wanted him to be a dead set winner every time he put the gloves on. That I always wanted a 99 per cent chance of success before I accepted a fight, that 50-50 would never be good enough. From then on, he never questioned one of my decisions and never tried to buck my system. What's more he'd start to sit down and talk to me more. It was no longer 'yep' and 'nuh' but he'd get me over to his place and tell me all about his past and the things he'd done wrong. He never tried to hide the fact that he'd been a real little lout. We've been close ever since."

Four days after that first ring frustration, all the pent-up anger was released in one furious round against Craig Easey's training partner Greg Ross, an unbeaten prospect who thought he'd clean up the young hood from Newtown. The fight took place in Canberra and Fenech's performance was straight from the school of dirty politics. The scales, perhaps unchecked for some time, showed Fenech weighing in at a career low 45 kilograms (just one pound above being a seven stone weakling), but the street fighter wasn't about to be the victim of any revenge pact. With each blow that Lewis watched his electric young protege deliver he became more convinced Fenech had the skills and attitude to be a really great fighter inside the ropes.

"They asked for the fight because they were sure their bloke would win well," Lewis said, "Jeff just belted him. Totally unbelievable. The way the kid was improving after just two fights! That bout set the pattern for the future. He just kept getting better and better. I don't think there's ever been a fight of Jeff's when he hasn't improved on the last time out. I've never had to say to him: 'Son that fight wasn't as good as your last'."

As every fight passed, Fenech's punches became more precise. His opponents suffered more. Soon Fenech was hitting to the body a little like Tony Zale, the Man of Steel, whose climb to the world middleweight title in the 1940s was brought about by what writer Red Smith called shots to the giblets so fearsome that they felt like red hot pokers thrust clear through the abdomen.

And so Fenech kept on the demolition trail, stopping Darren Berrigan in two rounds at Bronte in a fight that allowed him to score some sort of revenge for a fighter he idolised — Jeff Malcolm.

Two months before Fenech's third amateur fight, Malcolm, with visions of fighting for the world title and with Lewis in his corner and Fenech screaming his support from ringside, had lost a farcical contest with Berrigan's brother Peter, the Australian light-welterweight professional champion in their hometown of Newcastle. Veteran reporters called it the worst decision they could recall and it effectively ruined any chance

Malcolm had of meeting world champ Saoul Mamby.

Darren Berrigan gave up after two rounds of torture and a bite on the shoulder from Malcolm's young admirer.

In just his fourth amateur bout, Fenech was the NSW light-flyweight amateur champion having knocked out Craig Ison in one round, again at Bronte. He posed for a picture of triumph with Newtown team-mates Peter Mitrevski, who'd just taken the State flyweight title and Mark Cribb, who had claimed the bantamweight belt on the same program. But in the photograph, that now adorns the living rooms of both Fenech and Lewis, it's the fresh-faced light-flyweight who beams the brightest. He knew something the others only suspected.

But a world title was still a long way off, and before Fenech would even start dreaming about one, long before he would nearly give Satoshi Shingaki, Samart Payakarun and Victor Callejas brain damage, he would be beaten seven times as an amateur.

The first defeat came against flame-haired Joey Glover, a classy young boxer whose aged trainer Bill Boynton had predicted an Olympic gold medal, almost from his first victory 70 fights before.

Whenever Lewis has been in Fenech's corner, the Marrickville Mauler has won, inspired by the gentle reassuring words and the cold calculating tactical brain. It's been one of the best winning combinations in Australian sporting history. But in the days when Fenech was still exploring new territories as an amateur, Lewis was often overseas with Jeff Malcolm, looking for fights, often in futile, disheartening attempts to crack the American market. Lewis and his No. 1 professional were in Hawaii on June 24, 1982 when Fenech faced Glover at the Cronulla Leagues Club.

Fenech chased his opponent like a man running late for his first day of work, frantic beyond reason. With the same kind of weaving, darting style he would employ against Jerome Coffee three years later, Fenech received four cautions for ducking too low, a sin in the more rigid and disciplined confines of amateur boxing.

"Those four cautions lost the fight for me. In terms of points it was like Glover had hit me in the face, hard and clean 12 times," Fenech recalls, "If it hadn't been for the professional approach I took into the ring even then, he couldn't have beaten me. I was just making him miss the same way I make a pro fighter hit air."

That night Australian amateur hero Phil McElwaine and Tom Raudonikis, a titan of toughness, part-time pugilist, Police Boys' club patron and one-time half-back for the Australian rugby league team, were working Fenech's corner. Defeat left a rancid taste in Fenech's mouth. But he'd learned enough discipline from Lewis not to attack the referee and judges after the decision was awarded against him. For probably the first time in his life he restrained his aggression, biting into his swollen bottom lip and glaring menacingly when the winner's hand was raised. It was a look that said "I'll get you". And he did.

Four months later, four months in which he would see Glover's freckled face every time he punched a sparring partner or the padded targets Lewis uses to build a fighter's strength and endurance, Fenech had his revenge over the rival he hated most. Lewis, who arrived back in Erskineville in the interim to discover his boxer was no longer unbeaten, insists there was something faintly supernatural in Fenech's appearance before the return fight. Something indefinably frightening.

"He was so pumped up, it was scary. You looked into his eyes and all you saw was blind rage and determination. He'd grit his teeth and snarl and roar and I remember thinking that any minute he was going to rip into the first person who looked sideways at him. But he saved it all up for Glover and that night gave one of his best performances from those early days."

Fenech's initial preparation for the bout had been something of a disaster. Sandwiched between the two Glover fights was his second loss in just six fights, a setback that cost him any chance of representing Australia at the 1982 Commonwealth Games in Brisbane. He'd travelled to Hobart to lose on points against eventual national light-flyweight representative Greg Vanson. Fenech blamed poor advice from his cornermen. He'd been told to back-pedal from Vanson, to jab and move when he'd decided long before that aggression was the best form of defence. Under amateur rules, members of State and National teams would always be trained and seconded for representative contests by a designated coach. The designated coach was never John Lewis. Ultimately the decision to exclude the trainer from the corner from his most important bouts would cost Australian amateur boxing its brightest star.

After disposing of Glover in the return fight, Fenech would give Lewis an open show of the loyalty that has kept them together through thick and thin, despite the inevitable pressures created by an over-abundance of success.

After knocking out Warren Luland in three rounds in the rough and tumble western NSW town of Dubbo, Fenech, Lewis and others from the Newtown club who had driven the team bus up from Sydney, were attacked by a drunk wielding a broken bottle.

With murder in his eyes, the contents of the bottle and several others in his belly, and enraged by the bunch of laughing, celebrating city slickers, the drunk charged at Lewis, looking to open a few wounds of his own to get square for Luland's defeat. Off went the trainer and his fighters, running down the road with slurred, but blood-curdling threats driving them on. Finally, Fenech tired of running. The broken beer bottle gouged into his scalp, the blood seeping through his woolly hair and into his dark eyes. He responded by kicking the drunk's head into the gutter, then bouncing on his throat like a trampolinist. No one threatens John Lewis while Jeff Fenech is near.

Back in Sydney the fiery little street-brawler had established himself as a boxer of great promise, even among the amateur officials whose ears burned at his outright defiance of authority. He was already a boxer with a reputation. An opponent no one could take easily. Six months passed when Fenech couldn't get a fight. Six months when he'd watch his diet like a Weight Watcher of the year. Six months when he'd turn up at tournaments all over NSW but never see any action. Finally, in March '83, he faced up against Grant Richards, a ferret-faced storeman who worked in a Safeways grocery store in Melbourne and who had picked up a bronze medal as a flyweight in the Brisbane Games a year before. For three rounds Fenech tried to use Richards as a door mat until the bizarre ending which saw Richards counted out on his feet and Fenech disqualified for head-butting. Amid the confusion Australian amateur boxing chief Arthur Tunstall, one of the country's most senior amateur sporting officials, recorded the bout as a Fenech victory.

Two more wins, one of them over the wily Brian Williams (who would later become a sparring partner for the world champion) followed before Fenech won his second State title.

No one turned up to fight him. The victory over Williams, a fast, well-balanced, stand-up boxer, kept every capable flyweight away from the State championships. Fenech was now unbeatable on home soil.

The week before the championship, he had his first taste of publicity as an amateur boxer, shaping up with rugby league international Steve Rogers for a Sydney *Daily Telegraph* photograph. It was the first bite, and he liked it. Three more wins, each of them over tough opponents, gave Fenech his first Australian championship. At the Palais de Sport in St Kilda, Melbourne, he outpointed Tony "Mad Dog" Miller, from Western Australia, knocked out Grant Richards in a return bout and outboxed Queenslander Michael Fry to take the flyweight title with a left jab that was by now, almost a lethal weapon.

Applauding loudest in the crowd was the much loved trainer, who hadn't been allowed in Fenech's corner. But as he yelled himself hoarse from ringside, it was the only voice Fenech could hear. Now the fighter was ready for top-shelf opposition. Almost ready anyway. He took his first Oceania region gold medal by shoving a hot poker into the belly of New Guinean David Veali before outclassing tough Ashley Thorne in the NSW country town of Narromine. As part of Lewis' team, Fenech had already fought all over Australia, raising money for the air fares through chook raffles with his mum or helping with the navigation when Lewis would pack the fighters in to the team bus for tournaments at one-pub towns. Now he was preparing for his first big test. A test he failed.

In September '83 in trouble-torn Belfast, Fenech discovered that his own brand of terrorism still wasn't enough to outweigh the finer points of boxing at the first Commonwealth titles. Together with a new breed of Australian amateur fighters like Shane Knox, Renato Cornett, Brendon Cannon and Ricky Finch, who would all console each other in Los Angeles months later, Fenech was becoming a world-travelled athlete. Joey Glover was in Belfast, too, as Australia's bantamweight representative, but he and Fenech didn't talk much. Fenech picked up a bronze medal, but only because of the draw in the flyweight division. He lost his only fight at the tournament to local sensation Jerry Duddy, who in turn lost in the final against Patrick Clinton, who a year later at the Los Angeles Olympics, would be knocked unconscious by a quick little Yugoslav named Redzep Redzepovski.

Despite the loss to Duddy, Fenech refused to let remorse take control. He realised that no great gain could come without sacrifice. He knew there'd be fights he wouldn't win in his apprenticeship.

Going home through London, Fenech had newspaper headlines printed at a novelty store. "Fenech and Knox — Future World Champions". It was kids' stuff at the time, but within two years, Fenech had made it and Knox, an orphan trained in boxing by a kindly foster father in Brisbane, was well on his way.

Fenech was in love with boxing by the time he fought in Belfast. He was smitten. And there was no turning back. He didn't always win but he found the same delight in close combat as Joe Frazier did when he summed up the buzz by saying: "When I punch a fellow and see him crumble from the power of my hands and fall onto his back, I feel great excitement. There's a great thrill to it."

Belfast had been a disappointment. But Fenech's dedication and competitive spirit made him a favourite with teammates. Although he was one of the youngest and least-experienced of Australia's boxing internationals, he would be made team captain for Los Angeles. Intensity and self-promotion had done the trick.

Still denying himself the lollies, the milkshakes and potatoes he loved most, and gulping down laxatives to stay under eight stone, Fenech scored his first major international triumph in the quarter-finals of the World Cup in Rome one month later. There were great fighters to rub shoulders with and fight against. Russians and Cubans and Italians and South Americans like his quarter-final victim, a noodle-thin Colombian flyweight who stood a head taller than the Australian and had the reach to match. Although Fenech had been boxing for less than two years he already had the knack of beating opponents with better credentials. The Colombian could not handle Fenech's sustained pressure.

"In those days, I just had my strength and my left jab," says Fenech. "I still hadn't learned how to throw my other punches the way some fighters could. In Rome, I just made him back up with my jab and then got in close to hammer away. I got cautioned a couple of times, but I landed enough punches to win the fight well."

The win put Fenech into the World Cup semi-finals and

made him one of the world's top 10 amateurs in his division. But in his next bout, he ran face first into an opponent who would cause him the most trouble as an amateur, the multi-talented South Korean Heo Yung Mo.

Heo, a year older and with a 1981 World Cup silver medal to his long list of credits, was simply too skilled for a capable fighter, who by comparison was little more than a novice. Heo had the rapid-fire punching style that separates great amateurs from the rest.

With just a swivel of his shoulder and hip, Heo could fire three, four, five left hooks with a loose, yet elegant style that suggested every muscle and tendon was independent in his compact frame. He whipped Fenech in the semi-finals at Rome, taking a unanimous decision before losing in his second World Cup final against Cuba's little superman, Pedro Reyes, then favourite for the Olympic flyweight gold before the Communist boycott of LA was made known.

Heo had also staggered Fenech for the first time in his fighting career, landing a thumping left hook over the right temple on his way to a clear-cut win. Fenech had taken Rome more seriously than any prior tournament. He knew it would have a great bearing on his chances of fighting in LA and his mood before the World Cup tournament was far removed from the holiday atmosphere on the team bus in Belfast. He and Peter Mitrevski, who represented Australia as a featherweight, although really three divisions lighter, played pranks and gave team officials some anxious moments. When it came to the actual fighting however, Fenech was even more serious than for that "scary" return with Glover.

But more disappointment clouded Fenech's horizon. Six months later in the sweltering heat of Bangkok, Heo beat him again on points. Only this time it was closer and Fenech showed the little Korean that his rate of improvement was a challenge to be feared at the Olympics.

Heo was one of Fenech's finest teachers. The lessons the Australian learnt from Heo allowed him to win a second Oceania gold medal in Taiwan, and shrug off a hometown decision against local hero Sugiarto in Indonesia.

"Every time Sugiarto threw a punch the crowd would scream and cheer even if he missed," Fenech recalls bitterly. "All I could hear was a million of his mates yellin' "Nyah Nyah" for nine whole minutes. After the fight my cornerman Mick Canavan said if I didn't get the decision he'd run around the ring with no clothes on. They gave it to the Indonesian but Mick didn't get the gear off. I lost out both ways."

The only obstacle between Fenech and his subsequent selection for the LA team was an ageing amateur from a North Queensland Aboriginal mission. Depending on who you talked to, Danny Murgah was unbeaten in anywhere from 16 to 116 fights. He'd come out of retirement to go to Los Angeles, just like he'd come out of retirement for the Brisbane Games, only to think again, under pressure from other Aborigines advocating a political boycott. His Queensland team-mates said Murgah was a shock puncher who could dance your feet off for three rounds or break your jaw with either fist.

Things looked ominous when Murgah's best mate from the mission, southpaw Bertie Harris, smashed Australian champion and another Belfast medallist John Sutherland to the canvas in the opening round with the kind of punch Joe Louis would have been proud of.

John Lewis, watching in the crowd, swallowed nervously as he watched Fenech climb into the ring. He needn't have worried. Fenech walked through Murgah as though the Queenslander didn't even exist. It was February, 1984, and Fenech was guaranteed a place on the plane to LA. Sadly, there was to be no seat for Lewis.

Late in 1983, the trainer took Fenech and Mitrevski to Fiji to give his flyweight a better preparation for the Olympics. Fenech was far too strong for Western Samoan Lautapo Ofa Wong King. Lewis had no inkling of the furore that awaited them back home.

"We'd each spent more than $1000 to get there and the only reason we went to Fiji was to get Jeff some badly needed experience," says Lewis. "No one at home was willing to fight him and we had to look for guys who'd put up a good effort. So we all went out of pocket to get there. But the amateur officials in Australia said we'd had no right taking fights without their permission. They reprimanded Jeff and Peter and suspended me as a trainer for six months. It was the worst I've been hurt in boxing. Worse than when Jeff lost to Redzepovski. I felt dirty. From then on, I knew there'd never be any hope that Jeff and I could be together at the big tournaments. He tried to convince Arthur Tunstall and the other amateur people to let me go in his corner. Jeff had such faith in me and our bond was so strong, that no matter who else was in his corner and no matter what they knew, they just couldn't measure up to Jeff's expectations. From the time I got back-handed, the writing was on the wall for Jeff's amateur career."

Still Fenech had one goal to achieve before he threw away his green and gold singlet. It was something no Australian had ever achieved.

He wanted an Olympic gold medal in boxing. ■

8
An Olympic Nightmare

*"Sometimes people get hurt, but it does no
harm to be knocked out once in a while."*
Jack Dempsey,
heavyweight champ 1919-1926.

The 1984 Los Angeles Olympics represented a light at the end of a tunnel for Jeff Fenech. He just hoped that light wasn't a speeding train.

As it turned out, even a head-on confrontation with a locomotive might have been less agonising than the mental anguish that accompanied Australia's best boxing medal hope on the lonely and empty-handed trip home. The crunch for Fenech didn't come from the gloves of his three opponents inside the ring. It came from a series of setbacks, some of them self-inflicted, that conspired to change what should have been the most rewarding experience of his life into a nightmare.

Amateur boxing is hardly a high profile sport in Australia, even in an Olympic year, and the *Daily Telegraph* and *The Australian* were pretty much the only newspapers prepared to acknowledge Fenech's growing reputation. But their reports were enough to create a public awareness that Fenech was finding distinctly appealing. It felt good. The occasional kid pushing an autograph book under his nose and the drinkers at the Marrickville Hotel slapping him on the back and wishing him luck. But the euphoria didn't last long. Even though he enjoyed the growing recognition from people who knew nothing about boxing, but had been swept up in the fever that always leads up to an Olympics, Fenech knew his old sore with amateur boxing officials would continue to fester.

It wouldn't matter how modest he was, there could be no denying he was the only possible gold medal hope in the Australian team. At best, Renato Cornett, a flashy, slick-moving lightweight from Sydney's western suburbs, at 19 the second

51

youngest of the five Australian boxers chosen for the Games, was conceded an outside chance of winning a bronze medal. So was the team babe, 18-year-old Queensland featherweight, Shane Knox, but his task was to become so much tougher through the trauma that accompanied the death of the kindly retired policeman who had coaxed him from an aimless orphan existence on the streets of Brisbane and shown him a new road to hope through boxing. Like Lewis had done with Fenech, Sgt Nev Poppleton became a father figure as well as a fight trainer to Knox. But only a matter of weeks before the Olympic team was announced, Poppleton suffered a heart attack and died in his young protege's arms.

The other two members of the Australian boxing team, Victorian middleweight, Brendon Cannon, and Queensland light-middleweight Ricky Finch, were eager and game, but seemed to lack the credentials to survive beyond the elimination rounds of an Olympic tournament. Fenech knew he shouldered most of the responsibility in the quest for gold, a status his four team-mates openly acknowledged by electing him captain of the squad, although Cannon and Finch were both older and all four were more experienced.

The Soviet-inspired boycott of the Los Angeles Games removed one of Fenech's biggest hurdles, Pedro Reyes, Cuba's dual Olympic Gold medallist and the 1984 favourite. When the Cubans eventually opted to join a growing list of Communist stayaways from the 1984 Olympics, Fenech knew the flyweight division gold medal was within his grasp, providing he could improve enough to beat Heo Yung Mo. Known as Panface because of his remarkably flat facial features, Heo had been responsible for two of only six fight defeats Fenech had ever suffered, assuming that the smack in the nose from the seven-year-old schoolmate all those years ago didn't really count.

Beyond any doubt Fenech reckoned Heo was the man to beat for Olympic gold. With any luck he'd only have to take command of those nine hectic minutes, those three three-minute rounds against the sturdy South Korean, and Fenech could achieve what had eluded 63 Australian fighters — win a boxing gold medal at the Olympics.

Ironically, the closest any of his predecessors had come was the very first, the remarkably versatile Reginald "Snowy" Baker, still widely acclaimed as the best all-round sportsman Australia has produced. He had competed at State or national

level in 29 sports and had represented his country in five —
swimming, diving, water polo, rugby union and boxing. His
points defeat against the Englishman J.H. Douglas in the
middleweight final at the 1908 Games in London remains one
of the most rankling and strenuously disputed in the history
of Olympic boxing. But Snowy Baker's Olympic medal effort
had never been bettered, or even equalled, by an Australian
fighter at the Olympics. Indeed, apart from Baker's achievement, Australians had won only three bronze medals in Olympic competition — welterweight, Kevin Hogarth, at the 1956
Games in Melbourne, and bantamweight Ollie Taylor and
light-heavyweight Tony Madigan in Rome four years later.
Aside from Baker, Madigan and Jimmy Carruthers, a young
bantamweight at the 1948 London Olympics, were the un-
luckiest.

Carruthers, who was to become Australia's first universally
recognised professional champion with his whirlwind destruction of South African Vic Toweel in 1952, breezed
through the early rounds of the 1948 Olympic tournament at
the expense of a Canadian, then an Argentinian. But he had
suffered a severe gash over one eye in the second contest and
failed to clear a medical check for a quarter-final against the
eventual gold medallist, Hungary's Tibor Csik, the following
day. Madigan, eliminated on a points decision in a middleweight quarter-final in Helsinki in 1952, advanced even further as a light-heavyweight eights years later, only to run into
an American semi-final opponent named Cassius Clay. It ended in a narrow points verdict in favour of the black man
from Louisville, Kentucky, but the quality of Madigan's performance was to be endorsed many times over, when Clay,
whose religious convictions inspired a change of name to
Muhammad Ali, was to establish himself in the eyes of most
discerning critics, as the greatest heavyweight of all time.

In the wake of all these tribulations, Australia was still
winless in Olympic boxing finals and John Lewis made sure
Fenech was well aware how close he was to a place in his
country's sporting history. Without the Communist Bloc
countries to worry about, and particularly the Cuban chance
Reyes, Lewis soon convinced Fenech that his South Korean
nemesis was the only real hurdle between him and achievement that had escaped every aspiring Australian for 76 years.
"Beat Heo and you win the gold" was the message Lewis
drummed over and over into the ears of his young fighter. But

he could not quite give Fenech the one reassurance he most wanted to hear — that he would be there in his corner in Los Angeles.

Fenech had lost only six fights, the only six fights he'd had with a comparative stranger calling the shots from the corner. The only six fights he had without Lewis to comfort his nerves and point him in the right direction. For all their pleas and protests, Lewis and Fenech finally had to accept that they would be more than 15,000 kilometres apart when the Olympic medal would be decided. Even if he had the money to fly over independently from the team, Lewis would not be allowed to supervise his fighter's preparation or join him in the corner where he was so desperately needed. Lewis knew how hard Fenech had worked for his chance at a slice of sporting history. Up to four hours a day, seven days a week, for months on end. Never complaining whenever he was called on for that little bit extra, for those punishing vital minutes of overwhelming pressure when the body is begging, screaming out for mercy.

Outside of tangling with sparring partners, boxing training can be excruciatingly monotonous. That is why only the supremely committed can make it to the top — and stay there. Hour after hour of shadow boxing against an imaginary opponent. Of skipping until the temples twitch and the breath escapes in ever-accelerating gasps; of pounding the heavy bag until the knuckles and every muscle in each arm feel like they're ready to crumble; they all demand the utmost in discipline and commitment. As he flayed into that stubborn heavy bag in the gym, Fenech could see the features of Panface wincing. That was his inspiration, the spur that kept him going as Lewis repeated over and over, "Beat Heo and you win the gold." Every morning as the buffeting winds of winter ripped through his tracksuit, he pounded the picturesque pathways of Centennial Park, oblivious to the trees and ponds and those hardy ducks and swans that only glided out from the shelter of the reeds to look for food for their young. Every time he passed a jogger he could see old Panface and without any conscious effort, would step up his own pace another gear.

Lewis had not seen such single-mindedness in anyone before. "I knew if I was sick and couldn't get out of bed, Jeff would do what he had to do," Lewis recalls. "He wouldn't crib an inch. He'd go through the usual pain barriers just as if I was there urging him on." The gruelling routine was imperative, not only to ensure he was ready to make the profile of Panface even flatter. Fenech had a weight problem. He was still growing and filling out, yet if he were to be just a fraction over the 51 kg limit when the L.A. action was due to start in the last days of July, they wouldn't let him step into the ring. Had he been like the usual 20-year-old athlete and enjoyed a night out on the grog with his mates, the weight problem might have overwhelmed him, but in those days Fenech drank nothing stronger than Coke or orange juice, and much to Lewis' relief, was usually just as happy with a glass of water. But still he had to watch every morsel that passed through his lips. If he relaxed too often even his single-minded commitment might not have been enough to save him. In the months leading up to the team's departure for a training camp in Colorado Springs, Fenech and his portable bedroom scales were constant companions. Being unemployed during his preparation for the Games was a big help. He could train whenever it was needed and by now he had attracted enough supporters in the Marrickville district's business community to know he would not go hungry. Supporters, like Marrickville Hotel licensee, George Savvas, who was to become his first significant sponsor after the Olympics. Savvas allowed Fenech to run raffles in the hotel bar to raise enough ready cash to keep him from pinching what he needed.

But the idle time didn't stop his stomach begging for fuel. When he wasn't training, all Fenech could think about was a heaped plate of steaming spaghetti at No Names, a less than fashionable but generous establishment he loved to frequent with Lewis and the rest of the gang from the Newtown Police Boys Club. When he was issued with his Games uniform a week before the team was to fly out to training camp, Fenech was just like every other first-time Olympian. Back in his bedroom, away from prying eyes that might mock him, he slipped into the wattle gold blazer and grey slacks and approvingly studied himself in the mirror.

But having to leave Lewis behind was still gnawing away at his peace of mind. He knew how tough it would be without the man who had taught him everything he knew about ringcraft. He'd never needed help to look after himself on the streets of Marrickville, Newtown and Redfern, but Los Angeles without Lewis was a forboding prospect. A desert without a compass.

Apart from five fighters, the 1984 Australian Olympic boxing team had a section manager, Sol Spitalnic, a successful businessman from Doncaster, Victoria. They were to pick up their coach, a 34-year-old American, Ed Weichers, when they reached their USA training camp. Weichers was a former national collegiate boxing champion who had been coaching at the US Air Force Academy at Colorado Springs for the previous nine years. He had developed 18 amateur national champions and 47 All-American. But he was going to have to start from scratch with the Australians — an awesome task considering he had less than a month to get them ready for the biggest boxing showpiece at international level.

Fenech did not like Spitalnic, who had been the Australian team manager at the King's Cup competition in Bangkok earlier in the year. Spitalnic was an experienced administrator and was assistant general manager of the entire Australian contingent at the 1982 Commonwealth Games in Brisbane. Although Spitalnic had endorsed a highly democratic suggestion to let the five boxers choose their own captain, he was to be sorely disappointed if he was expecting some significant support from Fenech. From the start, Spitalnic insisted on being the sole spokeman for the boxing team. The fighters were not to speak to the press unless he was present or had specifically authorised an interview. To Fenech, his discipline was pedantic rather than constructive. And worse still, Spitalnic represented the Australian boxing authorities, who were sending him to the toughest test of his life, to be trained by a total stranger who didn't even know whether Fenech fought orthodox or southpaw.

Fenech set out to be as insubordinate as possible. He disliked Spitalnic and didn't try to hide it. What's more he had no intention of being gagged and letting the section manager pull the strings and do all the talking. Although he was prepared to hate Weichers just as much, he found the American coach to be "a really great bloke". Weichers was full of enthusiasm for his task from the outset, despite frequent reminders from many of his associates and friends that he might be undermining his own country's medal prospects. But for all his agreeable nature, Weicher's coaching style brought almost immediate rumblings of discontent from Fenech and his four team-mates.

They had arrived in Colorado Springs in the morning after the tiring flight from Sydney and Weichers had them in the gym immediately after lunch. "He bored it into us from the start," Fenech complained to Lewis that night in the first of dozens of long-distance phone calls he was to make to the only man who really understood him and all his foibles. From anyone less committed than Fenech the complaint would have sounded hollow to Lewis. But coming from him, the Sydney trainer believed every word. "It's all hard conditioning stuff," Fenech went on. "Up to five hours in the gym every day." In addition, Weichers was making the five Aussie boxers run between eight and 10 kilometres in the type of rarified mountain air that had caused the mighty Australian distance runner, Ron Clarke, to collapse during the 1968 Mexico Olympics.

Weichers taught Fenech many great boxing adages. Fenech scrawled them on paper to recite again and again in a mind that was already plotting a gold medal. "Kill the body and the head will fall", "Tough times don't last. Tough people do". Despite his toughness, though, Fenech almost failed to see out the distance under Weicher's training.

"All the boys were complaining, but Spitalnic wouldn't listen," Fenech recalls bitterly. "Ed simply had us doing too much physical stuff at a time when we should have been sharpening up and learning the tricks that would help us in the ring. But it was no good looking to Spitalnic for a solution. He simply didn't know what was needed. How he came to be put in charge of us I'll never know. He'd hardly seen any of us fight and wouldn't have had a clue how many bouts I'd had. He was no help to us at all. Just a pain in the arse who was getting on our nerves."

The anger that had been simmering in Fenech finally erupted on the eighth day of the training camp. Weichers had kept up the punishing training schedule, yet Fenech and Knox were still having problems with their weight. They stayed behind in the hotel while the others went to a restaurant across the street for their evening meal. Suddenly the anger and the hunger spilled over. The hairline Fenech temper that Lewis had kept on a safety catch for so many months was triggered off. From the time his team-mates had chosen him as their captain, Fenech was sure they were banking on his defiant streak. They knew if things were going wrong and they had problems, then he would be the one most likely to speak up to have it fixed.

"Come on!" he yelled to Knox, "I'm going over to the restaurant to have it out with that bastard." But for the timely intervention of Weichers, Jeff Fenech's Olympic medal chase

might have ended in that Colorado Springs restaurant and
Sol Spitalnic could have ended up in the casualty ward of the
Air Base Hospital. Fenech reckoned the discontent among his
four team-mates was so savage that only the respect they had
all developed for Weichers as a man had averted an open re-
bellion. As team captain, it was his responsibility to revive
morale. Otherwise they might all drop their bundle before a
blow was struck in anger inside the ring. Tact and restraint
were only words in the dictionary to Fenech at that stage. He
let fly with both barrels at the startled section manager, pouring out all the frustrations, punctuated by the sort of language that was the native tongue of the street gangs back
home.

The restaurant was crowded, but the silence was deafening.
"I'll send you straight home," Spitalnic spluttered. "Bewdy!
You do that. Put me on the first plane to Sydney," Fenech bellowed back. Then the captain of the Australian team decided
to express himself in the way he knew best.

He lunged at Spitalnic, grabbing him by the lapels. "I was
gonna belt him one, but Ed Weichers leapt up and grabbed me
from behind," Fenech recalled. "It was probably just as well
because I was wild enough to have put him in hospital. I went
back to my room and rang up Lewie and told him what had
happened and that I wanted to come home. John said it was
entirely up to me. That if I wanted to come home, I should just
go ahead and do it. But then he said if I could just stick it out
a bit longer and put up with what was going on he was sure it
would be better for me in the long run. He reminded me of all
the hard work we had done together. Talking to John made
me feel a lot better and the next day Sol came over and
apologised to me and later Ed took Shane and me for a drive
and told us we should both get drunk and forget about what
happened the previous night. We didn't get drunk, but we
agreed to put all the bad feelings behind us. From then on
things were a lot better, but Sol was still trying to be bossy
when he didn't really need to be. He just couldn't help himself, particularly when someone from the press was around.
He'd always be telling them what they could say and what
they couldn't say.

"But just when I was getting to the point where I could live
with his irritating habits, I picked up one of the Colorado
papers — I've still got it at home — and there was an interview with Sol, a complete bagging of our boxing trainers in

Australia. I got real dirty. We weren't supposed to talk to the press about anything and here was Sol giving them a real song and dance about how bad our trainers are back home. To me that was like giving John Lewis a big serve and there was nothing I could do about it."

Actually, there were a few things Fenech, the larrikin prankster, could do to square things up for Lewis. "To get even" as he puts it. Once training camp was over and the team was settled at the Olympic village on the campus of the University of Southern California, he found a pet shop in a nearby centre and bought a little brown and white snake and a mouse. These two hapless little creatures were to become the central figures in a terrorism plot against Spitalnic.

When Fenech confronted the section manager and showed him the snake with a mock-up mouse tail hanging out of its mouth, the reaction was entirely predictable. "Get it away from me, don't come near me with that thing," Spitalnic screamed. But that had been just the beginning. Fenech then swiped the manager's keys, turned his room upside down, then threw the snake into the shambles. Spitalnic was terrified and Fenech and his team-mates loved every minute of it. "We eventually took the snake out of his room, but we let Sol believe it was still in there," Fenech says. "For nights afterwards, Sol would come knocking on my door late at night wanting to know if the snake was still in there. I always pretended I was asleep."

The mood turned much nastier just before Fenech's first bout at the Olympics against Rene Centellas, of Bolivia. Without the calming influence of Lewis, Fenech was irritable and impatient. Olympic pressure does that to all competitors and Fenech was now phoning Lewis three or four times a day for therapy to his nerves. The calls always worked wonders for his morale, but not for Lewis' bank account as most were made reverse charges.

With the real business of fighting for medals already underway and Knox already eliminated on a borderline points decision by the Ugandan Charles Lubulwa, Spitalnic was being bossier than ever. All the five Australian fighters were quartered in one cramped room at the Olympic village and it didn't take much to touch off the biggest explosion of all from Fenech's already short fuse.

This time, he admits he went too far and was indeed very lucky not to have been sent home in disgrace without even touching gloves with an opponent in the ring. It happened in the team's quarters and Fenech recalls it this way: "It was just before my first fight at the Games and Sol was giving Brendon a hard time over something pretty trivial. I can't even remember what it was about. But I suddenly saw red and grabbed Sol by the throat and threw him to the floor. Then I picked up a table and tossed that on top of him. I was totally out of control. I jumped across his chest.

"If it hadn't been for Ed Weichers again pulling me back from behind I'd have belted the hell out of him. When it was happening, Sol didn't say anything to me. He just kept calling out for Ed to help him. All the other boys were cheering me on. I think they all wanted to jump in and help me. As Ed grabbed me away I remember screaming at Sol, 'Now you can send me home you f————.' When Sol left the room he was as white as a ghost and I thought to myself that I had really done it this time. But when I woke up the next morning Sol was standing beside my bed with a few hundred dollars for me to spend. He didn't say a word about the previous night. In fact he never mentioned it again. I'd really expected him to front up with the Australian team's general manager, Bill Hoffman, and my airline ticket to send me home. He only had to report what happened and I was a goner. That wouldn't have bothered me too much except that I was frightened that Johnny would never speak to me again. And without him there would have been no more fighting for Jeff Fenech."

Spitalnic may have been a constant source of irritation to his fighters; he may have been bossy and overbearing; but his manful silence about what happened that night deserved the respect of all who were privy to it. It was, after all, an unprovoked attack on a middle-aged man with no hope of saving himself from a severe beating, but for the timely intervention of the team trainer. Had Spitalnic wanted vengeance he only had to pick up the phone and Fenech's boxing future and public image would have been in tatters.

The assault on Spitalnic was not the only rush of blood Fenech suffered in the Olympic village. He chose a strange way of trying to cheer Knox up after the Queensland teenager's hairline points defeat against Lubulwa. "Shane was really down in the dumps because he thought he had done enough to win," Fenech recalls. "We all thought he had won too, but trying to console him only seemed to make it worse. He burst into tears. I decided to stick with him to give him some moral support and to convince him that he hadn't really let anyone down. We were just outside the stadium when a security guard pulled up on a motor scooter and left it with the engine running. Shane and I took one look at each other and then jumped on it and roared away. We'd only gone a couple of hundred yards when two highway patrol cops dressed just like in that CHIPS programme on television zoomed past us. I don't know how we got away with it. We must have looked ridiculous. There I was in my green and gold Australian tracksuit doubling Shane who was still wearing his boxing trunks, boots and singlet. When we got back to the village we hid the scooter and used it to get around downtown LA until we went home. I know it was a stupid thing to do and if we'd been found out we'd have been in big trouble. But our luck held out and I'm still wondering if the security bloke ever found the scooter."

But the luck didn't stick with the Aussie boxers in the ring. They all fought bravely and well but returned home without even a bronze medal to show for it. Shane Knox had to concede height and reach advantages to Lubulwa, yet he stormed home so strongly in the third and final round that the points verdict against him aroused prolonged jeering from the near-capacity crowd. Brendon Cannon was next man out, dropping a points decision to the rugged and unorthodox Canadian, Ricky Duff. Once again the crowd at the Los Angeles Memorial arena erupted in disapproval believing Cannon's spectacular final round comeback had earned him victory, proving yet again that in boxing last impressions are by far the most lasting and often most deceptive. Duff's power punching had Cannon reeling in the first two rounds and the referee had to apply the standing eight count three times on the Victorian. Somehow Cannon came out for the third round looking fresh and confident and shook the Canadian before battering him with two-fisted flurries. Weichers seemed to have worked a miracle in the 60 seconds between rounds. In that final session Duff was twice in desperate trouble after running into left hooks thrown with all the fire power Cannon could muster. Duff hung on to take a narrow points verdict. The Australian's great rally had come a fraction too late. Ricky Finch bowed out as nobly and if there was no real dispute about the decision in favour of Zambia's Christopher Kapopo, the voting was close.

The disappointment of the three beaten Australian fighters

was so overwhelming they decided to return home without waiting for the boxing tournament to end or for the Games closing ceremony, one of the highlights of the entire Olympic festival. They were hurting too badly inside to stay on in the village thinking what might have been. They hated to leave Fenech and Renato Cornett to battle on alone, but they knew the two surviving team-mates would understand.

Cornett was starting to shape up like a medal winner, his morale and confidence boosted by a close points decision over a crafty and vastly more experienced opponent from Romania, Viorel Ioana, who had won 200 of his previous 236 fights. The young Australian lightweight was even more convincing in his next bout, grafting out another tight points verdict over Herman Gutierrez-Zuninga, of Colombia. But with a bronze medal seemingly in sight, Cornett experienced the sort of heartbreak that Fenech would know only too well just a few days later. Cornett's third bout was yet another cliffhanger and despite the formidable credentials of his Korean opponent, Chil Sung Chun, three of the five judges voted in favour of the Australian. But a jury of five reversed the judges' by a 4-1 majority, leaving an embittered Cornett in tears, fearing his supporters at home might think he'd let them down. He had in fact fought well above his Australian form throughout the tournamrent and Chun went on to claim the bronze medal by eliminating a Filipino in his next fight.

And so it was left up to Fenech to fulfil the confident pre-tournament prediction by Weichers that he was clearly Australia's outstanding medal prospect and a genuine chance for the gold. Weichers was convinced the Australian team captain would be too strong and aggresive for the flyweight gold medal favourite, Steve McCrory, of the US. Fenech could hardly have been more impressive in whipping Centellas with the referee intervening in the third round to save the plucky Bolivian from needless punishment. The highpoint of Fenech's amateur career followed against David Mwaba, of Tanzania. Viewing the fight on television in his lounge room in Erskineville, Lewis was ecstatic as the five judges unanimously awarded the contest to his fighter. At that stage he was sure only Panface Heo stood between Jeff Fenech and Australia's first Olympic gold medal in the boxing ring. But Heo had broken his hand in a sparring session before the Games and, although he battled gamely through his first two bouts, he was bundled out in a quarter-final by the eventual bronze medallist Turkey's Eyup Can.

That surely left only McCrory as a genuine threat, although Fenech's phone calls to Lewis for reassurance were becoming increasingly frequent. He was having problems keeping his weight down and Weichers had him jogging through the streets of downtown LA trussed up in two heavy tracksuits, to stay within the 51 kg limit. Fenech was always hungry, but now Spitalnic was totally supportive and overwhelmingly compliant and he had come too far to let something as trivial as an empty stomach check his progress. The bronze medal was at stake in the next fight against Yugoslavia's power-hitting Redzep Redzepovski who had an awesome knockout record and had destroyed Britain's hope Patrick Clinton in the previous fight. Perhaps the Yugoslav's reputation influenced Weichers' pre-fight instructions. Fenech fought much too cautiously in the opening round. The tactics were hastily reviewed at the first break and Fenech, now convinced he could take Redzepovski's best shots without flinching, went after the Yugoslav. When the nine minutes of action were over, Fenech knew there would be very little between them on the judges' cards. He thought he'd just got there. The wait for the decision was excruciating. He dared not glance to the ringside enclosure where his sister Veronica was balanced on the edge of her seat. Suddenly the reformed dead-end kid from Sydney sensed the delay was a bit too long. It was to be another jury decision. Then came the announcement that left him numb with disappointment. The judges had voted in his favour 3-2, but the jury had reversed the decision by a 4-1 majority. Redzepovski was the winner, and would go on to the silver medal in a final split decision loss to McCrory. The jurymen were only called in when the judges were divided 3-2. They could only reverse a decision by a 4-1 or 5-0 majority. It was a new system at the Olympics and one that belied credibility. The original judges were all skilled and experienced men at assessing fights at international level. The jurymen were senior administrators who, irrespective of qualifications, were given the over-riding job, probably only to justify their presence at the Games.

As a vast majority in the hall responded to the jury intervention with sustained hooting. Fenech raised Redzepovski's right arm in a sporting salute. Then he hurried from the ring hoping no one could see the tears welling up in his eyes. He said nothing as Ed Weichers shook his head and whispered the prophetic words: "Someday kid, you're gonna be a champion". In the press interview room the composure cracked. The frustration and disappointment overwhelmed him. Fenech thanked everyone who had helped him along the way. When he mentioned Lewis' name he choked up. His voice broke and so did his self-control. He was crying now, but that didn't stop him launching a scornful tirade at "the senile old men" on the jury that had just deprived him of at least a bronze medal. Then he blurted out that he was through with the amateur fight game.

It was more a threat than a promise. He spat it out rather than said it. "That's it for me in amateur boxing. As soon as I get home I'm turning pro. They may have cheated me out of winning a medal at the Olympics, but they won't stop me from winning a world title for Australia."

If they had looked closely, the international pressmen who bothered to turn up at the stone-walled interview zone behind the fighters' dressing-room, would have noticed that Fenech's bottom lip was quivering. He had tears in his eyes, triggered as much by rage as by the disappointment. As usual, he was talking too fast to be clearly understood by the boxing writers from Yugoslavia, Korea, Mexico and half a dozen other countries where the English langauge was something they only grappled with at school. "I've worked so hard for the chance to win Australia's first boxing gold medal at the Olympics, only to have the chance taken away by a bunch of senile old men." The few Australian journalists in the interview room understood. So did the ones from Britain who had been tipped off to the tremendous potential of the fiery youngster from the grey streets of Sydney. But most of the sports writers in the room weren't too sure what to make of Fenech's passionate protest. To them he was just another sore loser and there had been plenty of those before him.

As Fenech cried, as much for his loyal trainer as for himself, Johnny Lewis flicked off the television set in his Erskineville home and shed a few tears himself. "Sure it was close, but I thought Jeff should have got the decision," the softly spoken trainer was to say later. "If ever there was one of his fights I was disappointed in, it was that one. I felt he should have summed up the situation a lot earlier. The Yugoslav bloke was dead set running on empty from the second round. Weichers should have summed it up sooner. That was the big problem. Weichers wasn't quite sure what Jeff was capable of

Above: Fenech has always had the benefit of good advice from people like Lewis and Pat Jarvis (right) the rugby league-playing policeman.

Below: At the World Cup in Rome, Fenech had the mateship of an old buddy, Steve Zines (centre) and New Zealand Olympic medallist Kevin Barry.

Even though the sight of Redzep Redzepovski with his hand raised made Fenech burn, he still applauded the winner of their controversial Olympic battle.

*John Lewis, in the proudest night
of his life, leaps into the ring as
Fenech flops to the canvas in
delight after beating Satoshi Shingaki.
— Photo Gary Graham, Daily Telegraph*

NSW rugby league skipper Steve
Mortimer became one of
Fenech's great friends and
biggest fans. Each inspired the other.

doing. You can't get to know a fighter in three weeks. Jeff should have walked right through Redzepovski ... knocked him out. It shouldn't have even gone down to the wire. When Jeff beat the Tanzanian, Mwaba, he beat the best fighter in the division. There's no doubt in my mind Jeff would have walked right through McCrory for the gold medal. If I'd been in the corner I'd have summed it up sooner. Redzepovski could punch hard, but he definitely wasn't fit. If Jeff had gone after him sooner, the bloke would have been a spent force in the third. What happened with the jury overturning the verdict was cruel. I doubt if there was a fighter at the Olympics who had worked harder for a medal for his country. The chance to work on one of those Olympic juries was just a reward, a perk for services rendered, a free trip overseas for the biggest parasite in the country. It would have taken only a couple of words from me in the corner and the judges and jury wouldn't have been needed. They could have sat back on their fat arses drinking their free beer."

Whatever Lewis and everyone else back home thought of the decision, Fenech was shattered. All the reformers had told him so often that good living and hard work always had their rewards. Apart from a few minor derailments like his run-ins with Spitalnic and the "borrowing" of the security guard's motor scooter, Fenech had stayed on the right track for almost two years. For what? The press interviews over, Fenech didn't even bother to take a shower or change back into his street clothes. He just wanted to get the hell out of the place, not only out of the stadium but out of Los Angeles, out of America and back to Australia and Johnny Lewis and the rest of his mates. Spitalnic, in keeping with their recent truce, was compassionate and understanding. Weichers was distraught. After throwing a consoling arm around the Australian fighter he had come to admire so much, he yelled to any pressman or fight official who would listen: "What happened out there to this boy was an absolute disgrace. It has no place in the Olympic Games and I am embarrassed such a thing could happen in my country."

But at the time Fenech didn't need to hear how unlucky he had been. That only made him want to cry some more. He desperately wanted to be alone for a while. Leaving his bag and street clothes on the dressing-room bench, he walked out of the stadium still in his boxing trunks and robe, ignoring the stares as he headed back to the Australian quarters at the

Olympic village less than a mile away. He ran a bath and soaked in it for hours, crying and thinking and fighting through those nine minutes with Redzepovski over and over again. He wanted to call Johnny Lewis, but decided this wasn't the time. His trainer and closest friend was probably hurting enough without hearing him cry over the phone.

The Olympic closing ceremony was only a matter of days away and he had heard that it was one of the Game's most sublimal experiences for the competitors. But he didn't want to be there, or at the Olympic boxing finals where he would see some fighter collect a medal that was righfully his. When he saw Spitalnic back at the village that night Fenech told him he wanted to be on the next flight home. "Don't try to talk me out of it, Sol. I need to get the hell out of here," he explained. "I might think differently later on, but right now the Olympics are just a disaster for me. I need to get back to Sydney and be with my folks and my mates." Spitalnic understood and booked him on a Qantas flight leaving the following night.

It's easy to brood on an international jet. All those hours strapped loosely in a seat with nothing to do but eat, sleep or watch a movie. Fenech didn't sleep or watch the movie. He just kept thinking about Redzepovski, that boxing jury and what they were all thinking back home. And he wondered if it had really been worth going straight and reforming, if this was the only type of reward he could expect. He thought about the next Olympics in Seoul four years away. He could prove them all wrong over there, but what if he was to run into another bunch of senile old men on the jury. He didn't think it was worth it and anyway, Johnny Lewis wouldn't be allowed near his corner. A pro career seemed the obvious choice and if he ever got the chance to fight for a world title it would be much fairer — one-on-one, experienced referees and judges and no juries. He also thought about those struggling turbulent years he had been through, when the law was his main opponent, and when he did most of the cheating. ■

9
The Club Fighter

"I don't want to knock my opponent out. I want to hit him, step away and watch him hurt. I want his heart."
                                        Joe Frazier, 1973.

BOBBY WILLIAMS was a clown, a real clown. In the dustbowls and isolated hamlets of New South Wales he'd made people laugh for months. A tiny little clown, whose face, already starting to show the wears of his boxing habit, bore greasepaint the way it absorbed Jeff Fenech's left jab. All over.

For 12 months, back in his struggling youth before his job canvassing for a paint company and working for the Penrith City Council, Bobby Williams had been a circus clown. He was paid to make people laugh.

They were still laughing on October 12, 1984, the night Fenech launched his career as a professional boxer with a two-round display of brute strength and cold-blooded malice that would become his trademark and leave wee Williams mangled on the canvas.

The more compassionate in the beery crowd of 300, scattered around the ring at long white tables from where every drop of blood was clearly visible, looked the other way. It was the only decent thing to do.

Friday night. Bobby Williams beaten beyond the limitations of his endurance and now placed before the crowd at the Marrickville RSL club and asked to explain what went wrong. With his ribs almost caved in, each breath Williams took only made him more pitiful and tragic. Each gasp of air crumpled his face into a mask of agony. Each attempt to speak gave the impression he would burst into tears.

"I've fought all over the world," Williams wheezed, one hand grasping a microphone as though it was a lifeline, the other feeling the cracks in his heaving rib cage.

"I expected the kid to start fast, but that second round was just incredible. I was confident of winning, but no one's ever hit me like that. Not even Frank Cedeno and he was world champion."

Bobby Williams was no big deal in the fight game. But he was tough and a crowd-pleaser. He left his provincial home in 1971 to join Sole Brothers Circus at the age of 15. He was fascinated with the gaudiness, the glitter, the exciting and the bizarre. It was a tough life, but he managed to work his way up from tent-hand to fully-fledged clown within a few months. He made them laugh wherever the circus took him and he was paid $20 a week to see Australia.

At 16, he started work in Bobby Tuite's travelling boxing troupe, punching on with drunks and local toughs in a thousand country towns where the black eyes and bruises healed long ago but where the experience lingers on forever. "I got five bucks a fight, and because I was the smallest bloke in the tent, everyone wanted to fight me. I figured I'd be better off in Sydney fighting in the real stuff. That was in '75."

Before his ill-fated fight with Australia's Olympic boxing captain under the dim lights at the Marrickville club, just around the corner from Fenech's home unit, Williams had done his best to hype the fight into a grudge match. The two had sparred long before the Olympics, and to anyone privy to the gym workouts, it was obvious that Williams' career was shaping up to calamity.

But he was being paid several hundred dollars in danger money, and what the hell, one good whack on Fenech's chin could have made him the most talked about boxer in the country. If he was scared, he certainly didn't show it.

"I started boxing when I was nine years old," he boasted before the bout. "That's about the time whatsisname was born. He's going to find out that this professional caper is a totally different ball game to the amateurs. I've had 30 fights as an amateur and 68 as a pro. I've been in with a world champ and I've fought for the Australian title four times. We'll see who's blowin' hard after round eight. I reckon Fenech will come out like a tornado in the first three or four rounds, but I plan to weather the storm. Ten rounds suits me down to the ground. There might be big wraps on the kid, but as far as I'm concerned, he's an unproven fighter. In boxing the older you get, the smarter you get. Fenech's never been past three rounds in his life."

That record was to remain intact. In the dressing room he shared with Wilma the stripper, before the bout, Fenech was throwing the hardest punches of his life against his mirrored image.

As the well-worn familiar theme from Rocky blared through the club's loudspeakers, he was building up his manufactured hate as he donned the same green and gold gown he'd worn the night he lost to Redzep Redzepovski, and even though he didn't say as much, it was obvious that in his first fight since the Olympics, he would never be so frustrated again. Ever!

It wasn't so much a fight, as an exhibition of Fenech's ferocity and determination. He was relentless, hammering Williams whenever and wherever he wanted. He needed three knockdowns to win — his punching power was still developing — but he was unstoppable.

He strutted around after the fight as John Lewis, the ringside doctor, and Williams' trainer Ray Wheatley rushed to the aid of his semi-conscious and badly hurt prey.

Fenech held his hands above his head, punching them towards the gaudy mirrored ball that hung above the auditorium dance floor. He looked across at the little clown. He smiled. The smile that would crack his hating face every time he won.

Fenech's professional debut had been a great start, but in terms of financial return, it was a disaster. The promoter of the bout, a gregarious former heavyweight champion, John McColl, expecting 1000 people to see the much-publicised Olympian have his first taste of fighting for money, drew less than a third of the expected gate. And lost money. It was only six months before Fenech was to draw a record crowd to his demolition of Satoshi Shingaki, but just then he was anything but a national celebrity. He had to keep winning and that was his only priority.

Fenech fought his first three professional bouts at Marrickville. None of them drew great crowds, and although he was constantly improving and winning with the brisk flourish and unemotional detachment of a hangman used to the noose, there was really nothing to suggest he was headed for fame and riches. Yet both were only a matter of weeks away.

John thought such heady days were still a long way off.

"I never had the foresight to see that Jeff could do so much so soon. Back then, I don't think anyone did, not even Jeff. I always wanted him to become Australia's first Olympic gold medallist. I knew he'd be unstoppable within six months after Los Angeles. That no amateur in the world would be able to stay with him. We might have lost it in Los Angeles, but there's no way we'd have been beaten in Seoul. If the amateur powers had let me go in Jeff's corner, he'd still be fighting amateur. But their loss was professional boxing's gain.

"After Jeff came back from LA he was bitterly disappointed. I took him to Fiji for three weeks for a holiday and to talk things over. I really wanted him to stay an amateur. A friend of mine was willing to give him a good job and provide him with all the time in the world to train for the Edinburgh Commonwealth Games and the Olympics in Seoul. But even before he left LA he'd made up his mind that he wanted to turn pro. I tried to talk him out of it, but he always wanted me in the corner. Looking back, you'd have to say he really made the right decision."

Through Lewis, Fenech was introduced to his first manager, Colin Love, an urbane Sydney lawyer. Lewis had been friends with Love for years.

"I met Colin through his brother George who was one of the nicest blokes I've ever met. I knew Colin had the same qualities, and being a successful lawyer with a whole range of important friends in business and sport, I knew he was the man to manage Jeff. We'd talked about bringing over a Kenyan flyweight called Steve Muchoki years before, but nothing ever eventuated. I told Colin that with his help, Jeff could be the biggest thing Australian boxing had ever seen.

"I made sure Jeff had all the physical and mental capabilities to win a world title and Colin secured the best possible deals for him. He did a tremendous job. He made sure all we had to worry about was winning."

Despite the publicity surrounding the heartbreak of Los Angeles and Fenech's chagrin with the mechanics of amateur boxing in Australia, he was anything but an overnight sensation as a pro.

Such was the meagre turnout to Fenech's paid debut that McColl scheduled his second bout against a stringbean from New Guinea, Percy Israel, as a preliminary contest, the first and only time that Fenech was not the main attraction on a professional boxing card.

Israel fell just two weeks after Williams. He stood more than six feet tall, had been fighting in the heavier junior lightweight division in Brisbane and was unbeaten in four fights compared to Fenech's one.

There was a far bigger crowd this time. This was attributed to the main event between two hulking cruiserweights, who abandoned any semblance of style for chin-slamming, rib-crushing roundhouse swipes.

Geoff "Iron Man" Peate, a part-time paratrooper and avocado farmer from Lismore, described by the ubiquitous and aliterative ring announcer Ray Connelly as "that human detonator of raging bombardment" and Daniel "Crusher" Saylor, a north Queenslander living in Sydney, who was a man "swearing allegiance to gladiatorial requirements" traded blow for sickening blow, spurred on by the hundreds, baying for blood. Peate finally stopped the exhausted, but defiant Saylor in six of the most savage and nauseating rounds ringside fans could remember.

On the undercard, Fenech baulked and feinted and crashed home punches all over Israel's skinny target area until referee Billy Males stopped the bout in the seventh. He overcame Israel's considerable advantages in height, reach and weight, giving the same kind of relentless, punishing performance that would characterise the first Shingaki fight. Everywhere he saw skin, he punched, until Israel lay against the ropes, his skeletal arms no longer able to throw back blows, but merely tucked against his ribs trying to minimise the constant buffeting.

Two weeks later Fenech travelled to Melbourne to fight his old amateur rival Tony Miller, the West Australian who had come to the Victorian capital as a sparring partner for his friend Lester Ellis. Miller was expected to be a dangerous opponent for Fenech.

Lewis realised Miller would be a risk, but labelled him "a one-pace fighter who was easy to hit". As far as Fenech was concerned, he was being paid $5000, more money that he'd earned in his first three fights put together, and since he'd already beaten Miller in the amateurs, he could just as easily do it again.

But the fight didn't come off. Miller weighed in above the agreed limit, prompting Lewis to call it off and head for home. Miller would later complain that he'd had the flu and that he would have made the weight if given another opportunity. But

Lewis was having none of it. That night, Ellis captured a disputed decision over Zambian John Sichula to launch himself into a world title fight with Korean Hwan Kil Yuh.

For the vacant Australian super-flyweight title, Fenech's third fight, two weeks later, was a one-sided shellacking of the smaller but highly regarded Queenslander, Gerald "Junior" Thompson, a former national light-flyweight champion, who had broken both legs when hit by a car as a kid, but who had later developed a small bodybuilder's physique.

Fenech had gone through just 13 rounds of pro boxing to claim the Australian super-flyweight title, a division largely unrecognised in Australia, but still a claim legitimate enough for him to boast of winning a national championship in only his third fight.

Lewis decided to take his fighter on another Fijian holiday. The Pacific playground is Lewis' second home and he thought his boxer could do with a well-earned rest. Maybe he could tee up a local promoter and get Fenech a few hundred dollars for a bout while they were there.   The Sydney youngster, who would soon be topping the gate takings of Sinatra and Springsteen, flattened Ilesia Manila before a handful of spectators at Suva's National Gymnasium a week before Christmas of 1984. Manila's muscular body looked menacing, but he went down from a single right hand and didn't move for five minutes. Fenech had warily boxed the renowned hard-hitter in the opening round and let fly with one numbing right early in the second. Until he iced Argentina's Osmar Avila in less than a minute three years later, that win was Fenech's only one punch knockout victory.

The promoters had lost money on the Manila fight and Fenech had been paid barely enough to cover his airfare and accommodation on his working holiday. But news that would change his life was waiting back home.

The week after Christmas the Sydney *Daily Telegraph* newspaper reported that Melbourne businessman Cos Sita was arranging a world title fight for Fenech against Japan's Satoshi Shingaki to be fought in Melbourne on February 22. The bout was planned as part of the undercard to Lester Ellis' IBF title-winning performance against the Korean with the worrying name, Kil Yuh.

Ultimately Lewis decided that Fenech should wait a few months and that Shingaki, whoever he was and whatever he'd done, could wait that long. ∎

10
A Star Is Born

"Boxing is show business with blood"
David Belasco,
US entrepreneur, 1915.

Jeff Fenech grew up believing he would have to steal life's privileges that others merely worked for. That all changed when John Lewis threw him the lifeline. Fenech, who was still only 20 when he won his first world title and the money and acclaim that inevitably went with it, was adamant, even during his LA Olympic campaign, that he wanted to be finished with boxing by the time he was 24. "I don't want to finish up with a flat nose and scars around my eyes," he would say. "I don't want to have my brain scrambled or shape up every time a glass breaks on the floor in a pub."

That's all very noble and very sensible, but boxing records are strewn with pathetic stories of young men who started off with similarly rational ambitions and finished up in the gutter or a pyschiatric centre, or even a slab in the city morgue, when they should have been enjoying the dividends of their accomplishments. The dangers of instant wealth, fame and glamour are as cancerous as they are profound.

A kid from the slums, as champion fighters inevitably are, suddenly discovers his fists can hitch him a quick ride on the roller-coaster to the top. People who didn't want to know him when his pockets were empty and his profile anonymous, except perhaps on police records, all want to be around him, particularly when the television cameras are whirring and swarms of admirers are pressing in. When such a kid finds he can earn money faster than the country's head of state, the temptation is there to spend it even faster. After all, he thinks, there's plenty more where that came from. What's $100,000 when you can pick it up for less than an hour's work in just one night? Or he can shake hands and kiss a few babies in a shopping mall for more money than the average man can earn in a month.

Sadly, apart from a vast minority who stick to the game plan and brush off the hangers-on to leave the profession with their earnings and faculties intact, the rest find themselves still on the roller-coaster on the way down. It always seems to end the same way. As time rusts once precision workings of the body and repeated concussions of the brain slow its messages, the champion inevitably finds himself confronted by another hungry kid with all the advantages of a new engine. And once the title goes, the ex-champ finds plenty of breathing space in his dressing room. This time, the crush is across the hall, where the fickle are acclaiming the new model. Apart from the consoling arms of his trainer and manager, there is nothing left but bitterness.

To guard against such a sadly, typical ending, Fenech had for his first title fight the integrity and staunch affection of Lewis and Love, whose job was to put black figures in Fenech's bank account once he had dropped the honour and glory ranks. Although Love had long been one of Lewis' closest friends, he knew virtually nothing about the fight game. But he had built up quite a reputation as a persuasive and convincing negotiator in legal and business dealings, particularly in sports-related activities. His experience in horse racing and rugby league football negotiations became widely known in Sydney after another close friend, Jim Comans, retired from full-time legal practice, but retained a high-profile public image by heading up the Australian Jockey's Club and the New South Wales Rugby League's affairs in judiciary matters.

Love didn't need to know the difference between a southpaw and a paw paw to steer Fenech and Lewis in the right direction. Lewis could handle the boxing. What he and Fenech needed most from Love was the quickest and least complicated path to a world title shot and the sort of investment advice people need when they suddenly come into a lot more money than they've been used to. The results he achieved were spectacular.

Fenech became the International Boxing Federation world bantamweight champion in his seventh professional contest and only 196 days after accepting his first pay cheque for demolishing Bobby Williams. In a gesture of gratitude and acknowledgement of Love's contribution to the greatest night of his life, Fenech kissed his manager's hand within minutes of taking Satoshi Shingaki's world title. Love had leapt from his ringside seat and reached through the ropes to shake hands with the new champion. He looked a trifle confused and embarrassed by this spontaneous show of affection from a young man who was once more used to mugging people than kissing them.

"I'm certain Jeff couldn't have climbed anywhere near the heights he has without Col there fighting it out for him in the boardroom," Lewis says. "He decided to manage Jeff just as a favour to me. It was a wonderful partnership."

But even Love's brilliance as a negotiator could not have steered Fenech to the world title as rapidly without the promotional flair of Bill Mordey, a Sydney sports writer turned publisher, who had been associated with the fight game for more than 25 years, and who among other reporting assignments, had travelled with Tony Mundine to Buenos Aires in 1974 for his vain assault on the great middleweight Carlos Monzon.

Mordey had long enjoyed a certain notoriety as a charismatic gambler and even if he drew the line at the traditional Australian folk lore reputation for supporting one of two flies on the wall, he was well known to have borrowed the cab fare home on more than one occasion from Randwick racecourse, the baccarat game at King's Cross or Thommo's two-up school.

Colin Love knew it would take a gamble to get Fenech's career rolling. After all, the young Marrickville Mauler's greatest claim to fame had been the highly controversial defeat at the LA Olympics and the Australian sports public had built a cynical attitude toward the fight game after a sequence of highly-publicised mis-matches. Mordey, a colourful 48-year-old, one-time council alderman and full-time punter, was ready for that gamble.

Known around Sydney as "Break-Even Bill" because of his constant claim that he only ever wanted to "break even" from his fight promotions, Mordey had the background, the contacts and the imagination to realise Fenech could mean big business. As a boy, Mordey was groomed to be a Catholic priest, but things didn't work out the way the nuns had planned. Many say his personality was moulded on the late Harry Miller, the long-time promoter at Sydney Stadium where boxing was a big money-spinner every Monday night.

Gambling and Mordey have always been eager bed-fellows.

"I've turned a little into a lot and vice versa, and I've walked home from every racetrack in Sydney," Mordey admits with a degree of pride. "It's amazing what you can do with luck."

When Mordey first became interested in promoting Fenech, he agreed to accompany Love and the rest of the Fenech entourage to the Dapto Leagues Club, near Wollongong, on the NSW coast for what was to be Fenech's fifth professional bout against the national flyweight champion and NSW bantamweight titleholder Wayne Mulholland, a home-town boy better known than the local mayor. Peter Fuller was the promoter, Mordey a sceptical observer.

Mulholland, a 25-year-old crane driver with 200 amateur and professional fights to his credit, dismissed Fenech before the fight as "unproven". Fenech predicted that his own strength, fitness and constant aggression would overwhelm Mulholland.

"Some people make their living by working in offices or factories. I make mine by being fitter, stronger and tougher than the people I fight," Fenech said, by now, two fights away from winning a world title. "You have to be positive if you want to get anywhere."

Mulholland, despite clutching on to Fenech for dear life throughout the fight, was unable to turn back the wave of punches that swept over him from the opening bell. He was beaten within five rounds.

Fenech finished with another scalp, Mulholland with a headache and a performance that Indonesian promoters decided made him a suitable victim for their world super-flyweight champion Elly Pical six months later. Mulholland lost that one in three.

The Dapto fans, spurred on by patriotic fervour, finished with bruised egos and empty pockets. Mordey finished with the resolve to breathe new life in to a sport that was clearly approaching its death throes.

On the way back to Sydney, Mordey, Love, Fenech, Lewis and about 20 friends who had been close to the cause for some time, pulled into a motel where the staff had agreed to stay back and cater for a late, but enthusiastic, victory dinner.

Mordey's first promotion on Fenech's behalf involved Rolly Navarro, a Filipino, short on stature and even shorter on talent.

Originally the opponent was to be a Mexican-American

called Carlos Conthola, who Mordey said was "a super-quick walk-up fighter". But it transpired that Carlos was more Mexican than anything else and not quick enough to elude the American immigration authorities, who regarded him as an illegal alien. Rolly Navarro was the substitute. Twenty-four hours before they left Manila for Australia, Navarro and his trainer Grego Garcia believed they were heading for a ride on the monorail past Mount Fuji. As far as they knew, the fight was in Tokyo against someone called Jeff Fenech. Garcia had been offered the fight by an agent in Tokyo acting on Mordey's behalf. The agent had forgotten to tell Garcia that the fight was in Sydney.

Navarro, a broad-shouldered southpaw in his mid-20s, came to Australia claiming a record of 32 wins from 42 fights. Garcia, who a month later would take the dangerous Rod Sequenan to Melbourne for a world title fight with Lester Ellis, said Navarro was a boxer, not a fighter, with only three knockout wins to his credit.

"He wins his fights by skill and courage. Last year, Rolly fought the IBF world super-bantamweight champion Ji Won Kim, and although he was knocked down in the second round, he climbed up and finished all over Kim in the last three rounds. Kim's face was covered in blood."

As well as brawling in the shameful infernos that pass as boxing stadiums in the Philippines, Navarro had previously fought in Japan, Thailand and South Korea. He was a world-travelled tough. Even though Navarro was described as looking like he'd fallen off a charm bracelet, Dapto promoter Fuller urged Lewis to pull Fenech out of the fight. He warned the trainer that the Filipino was dangerous. But the fight went ahead and was a bore.

In the opening round it became obvious that whatever Navarro's reputation back home, in Australia he was either homesick or hopeless. After the first round Lewis told his fighter: "Hold this bloke up for a while. We need some experience. Get some rounds." After three rounds Fenech, hyperactive until the day he dies, couldn't resist, couldn't wait any longer. He went after Navarro with that murderous look in his eyes.

Navarro fell in four. He might have been able to get up as Paul Moore counted him out, but what was the use. There was so much more of the same hurt if he had. Fenech suffered nothing worse than bruised knuckles as he demolished the little bloke with the porous defence, minimal attack and hard, hittable head. For Navarro it was more of a fright than a fight.

Mordey had staged the bout at the Hordern Pavilion, Sydney's most important indoor arena in the years between the time Sydney Stadium was demolished and the Sydney Entertainment Centre opened for business. He needed at least half of the 5000 seats to be filled, and even though there was still plenty of room in the stadium where Jimmy Connors and John McEnroe had battled so often at tennis, the crowd of 3500 was a tribute to the flood of pre-fight publicity Mordey's contacts in the media had helped to generate.

Fenech's close friend and namesake Joe Fenech had died only days before the fight. The elder brother of South Sydney rugby league club's captain, Mario Fenech, had been electrocuted while working as a plumber. Jeff was numbed and distraught. He dedicated whatever he might accomplish against Navarro to the memory of his mate.

As he demolished Navarro, the boxing experts in the crowd, most of them specially invited by Mordey to add some atmosphere and occasion to the one-sided fight, had diverse opinions about the kid from Marrickville and his record of six knockout wins in six fights.

Jimmy Carruthers, who had offered Fenech advice and encouragement throughout his amateur days, said: "He's a great fighter in the making. I was very impressed. What a straight left. But he's still got a long way to go." Johnny Famechon, the former world featherweight champion said: "A very good fighter but, after all, he had nothing to beat." Tony Mundine: "Fenech still has a lot to learn." Rocky Gattellari, who fought for the world flyweight title in the '60s: "It's madness to talk of a world title fight. He's three years away from a title." Tommy Burns, matinee boxing hero of the '40s and '50s: "A great prospect — but I've had tougher gym spars than that fight" and Vic Patrick, four decades before, the most beloved fighter in the country: "If he was really ready for a world title fight, he should have stopped Navarro in the first minute."

The sceptics remained. But they were all ready to come back and see Fenech fight again.

Mordey and Love knew the Hordern Pavilion would be jammed if they could lure Shingaki there for a title defence. ■

11
Local Hero

The Marrickville Hotel had never seen anything quite like it. Standing on the bar was a slender, suntanned young man who had terrorised the suburb for years. He was surrounded by thousands of luminous faces and eager hands slapping his muscular back. The hoodlum made good.

There were old faces beaming, like they had decades ago watching the likes of Vic Patrick, Tommy Burns and Freddie Dawson. Strictly working-class battlers who had seen one of their own become a national idol. Battlers, who had probably shuddered a few years earlier when they had seen Fenech coming to play with their children. Now they were kissing him, shaking his hand, wanting his autograph. There were kids there too, in their "Jeff Fenech sponsored by the Marrickville Hotel" t-shirts Lewis had designed to make his fighter some extra pocket money. Kids who had seen a real life Rocky story unfold before their young eyes and were already elevating Fenech to the status of a neighbourhood demi-god. The din of the crowd was stoked by the adulation. And they had enough steam up to last them through the next morning.

It was near midnight and outside on the footpath, under the glare of street lights and the countless camera lenses, masses were pouring through the pub door. And not just because the beer was free. Those who couldn't get in, swigged from cans and bottles and peered over a forest of shoulders for a glimpse at what was the most exciting thing that would ever happen to them. They had been part of one of the great stories in Australian sport. A story that through re-telling and editing would become more and more enthralling with each roll of the presses.

"Shit, who'd have thought he could do it," said unashamed Fenech fan Brian McCluskey, "I used to lock up the kids when I'd see him in the distance. Now he's made the whole country so bloody proud."

A few years earlier Fenech had been the pub's glass washer and resident loud-mouthed make-a-buck schemer. He liked hanging around listening to stories of big bets and bad blues. He liked rubbing shoulders with hard and devious men and there were plenty in Marrickville to keep a wide-eyed kid buzzing with stories that crime sometimes did pay.

Now Jeff Fenech was the one everybody listened to. The star attraction. He was standing on the public bar, a few thousand dollars worth of gold flashing from his chest. Around his neck were the bright, almost fluorescent, yellow boxing gloves he'd used to sever Satoshi Shingaki from his title and around his waist was the glistening red and gold world title belt — his scalp from the battle and his ticket to easy street. He was wearing a pair of running shoes, one of the hundreds of pairs he would be given by Asics Tiger, and grey and yellow beach pants acquired at cut price after he'd promised to give the shop assistant a plug on TV. Already Fenech, street kid forever, had learned the benefits of being in the public eye.

But if his pants were discounted, there was nothing cut price about the celebration. Fenech had just bludgeoned his way to the IBF world bantamweight title by punching-out Shingaki in nine one-sided rounds at the Hordern Pavilion.

As was to become the expected with Fenech fights, the bout broke all existing box office records, eclipsing the hall's best gate of $120,000 set by the old smoothie Frank Sinatra back in 1974.

Probably the kindest thing that could be said about Shingaki was that he seemed like a nice guy. As a world boxing champion, he was like a beaten up Volkswagon trying to win at Le Mans. He was tough and willing with a hint of style, but at no stage during his first fight with Fenech did the tall, spindly man from the ancient Japanese centre of Nara City, ever look likely to win. He never even came close.

The new world champion was now leading the Marrickville Hotel revellers in a rousing rendition of "Happy Birthday".

Many at the pub were drunk with celebration, others in-
toxicated by the excitement. Con Spyropoulos had turned 22
and was trying to blow out the candles on his birthday cake.
Con is mentally retarded and on the night of Jeff Fenech's
title win, he was probably the happiest young man in town.
Fenech was pouring foaming champagne over Con's balding
head.

In the weeks leading to the Shingaki fight, Con had helped
convince an army of dubious parents that Jeff Fenech was
really a heck of a nice kid.

Why, he seemed to say, if Fenech can count a retarded
young Greek as his best mate, then he must be worth supporting. Con helped de-brutalise boxing and increase its audience
to a whole new sector of the public which had probably found
it demeaning, archaic and abhorrent. The birthday cake and
champagne shower was Fenech's way of thanking someone
who, without even knowing it, had done a public relations job,
which the finest professional consultants would have had difficulty matching.

For the majority at the pub on the night of April 26,
Fenech's victory had been a monumental and euphoric upset.
For Fenech the result was never in doubt. Not from the time
he first saw Shingaki in action.

"I'll bash him", he liked to boast every time he'd show
someone the tape of the Japanese champion's first title defence in August, 1984. "See how he opens right up when he
gets someone hurt. All I have to do is fall back into the ropes
and he'll come at me wide open. I'll tear his head right off."

Fenech didn't need to fall back into the ropes or fake injury
against Shingaki. From the time the shy and pensive Japanese champion arrived in Sydney, it was obvious Fenech's
was the superior will, the superior confidence. He not only
dominated Shingaki in speed, strength and physical dimen-
sions, but his very presence was intimidating.

Shingaki arrived in Sydney five days before the fight. He
was dressed in a dark suit and a tie. He could have easily convinced the Sydney public he was a Sunday school teacher. His
pale complexion was of the same hue as the finest Japanese
porcelain and his long, angular body, as thin as bamboo
shoots, looked ready to snap at any moment. He could have
been taken for some junior executive with an electronics firm.
Maybe a young marketing consultant or a trainee stock-
broker.

He held a samurai sword above his head for the benefit of the cameras, but all the while he had the expression of a six-year-old waiting for the dentist to rip out a couple of molars. Shingaki had held the IBF bantamweight title for 370 days. When the newly-formed International Boxing Federation decided to thumb its nose at the more established World Boxing Association and World Boxing Council, Shingaki was selected to fight for their vacant bantamweight title. He'd only had a handful of bouts and 16 months earlier, had been stopped in 12 rounds by IBF junior-flyweight champion Dodie Boy Penalosa, of the Philippines.

Perhaps the fact Shingaki's promoter, cornerman and adviser, Hisashi Ikeda, was the vice-chairman of the IBF championships committee had something to do with his fighter meeting little-known Filipino, Elmer Magallano, with the vacant IBF bantamweight title at stake.

And so Shingaki, a southpaw with a minimum of defence and a maximum of heart, found himself in Australia ready to fight someone of even less experience — a boy who had boxed just six times as a professional for a grand total of 24 rounds.

Shingaki and his handlers arrived in Sydney with a sparring partner, Shinobu Kawashima, who had done the champion's confidence the world of bad by being knocked rotten in three rounds in a world title fight just two weeks earlier. The defeat should have been a terrible omen to the senior members of the Ikeda Boxing Club, but they had already decided $60,000 in tax-free American currency (the equivalent of $170,000 in Australian currency before tax) was a suitable incentive for their man to risk his crown against someone they considered to be nothing more than a well-promoted novice.

After all, Shingaki had been dodging undefeated American contender Jerome Coffee for more than 12 months and a tough but limited comer like Fenech was just the hit-out their fighter needed before meeting the much more ominous deputy sheriff from Nashville, Tennessee.

Shingaki's first public appearance in Sydney was at a rugby league match just hours after his jet from Tokyo touched down on April 21.

Obligingly Shingaki and his entourage tramped through the mud at Brookvale Oval, the home stadium of the Manly Sea Eagles in a northern beach suburb of Sydney. The Sea Eagles were playing the Balmain Tigers in a rain-drenched Winfield Cup match which served only to bemuse the fighter and Mr Ikeda, dressed in white suit, white shoes, white tie and looking every inch like a muddied Chinatown gangster.

It was Shingaki's first sample of the Australian public and the Brookvale fans who politely clapped the 21-year-old titleholder would soon be clamouring for his blood. Shingaki may not have understood the multi-legged sumo shape of the rugby league scrums, but he was well aware he'd be a lot more popular in Australia if he finished the title fight flat on his back. His nervous twitching and blinking, something Fenech would constantly mock, worsened as the days went by.

Three days before the title fight, Shingaki gave his only public sparring session, working out with the weak-chinned Kawashima, who shouldn't have gone anywhere near a gymnasium after his canvas sweeping in Korea. He also boxed one round with Lawrence Dapra, a 15-year-old high school student from Waverley College, who would spar several Fenech opponents in the months to follow. Hardened boxing men had heard about keeping champions in cotton wool. But this was ridiculous.

"He's supposed to be the bloody champ and they're putting in a little kid with him," one boxing writer said, shaking his head in disbelief.

It was explained Shingaki was just going to "move around". Just limber up his muscles against some sort of moving target. The reporter shook his head again. To him Shingaki was already a bum.

The champion boxed within himself against Dapra as Jack Dempsey, Freddie Dawson and Cassius Clay looked down from portraits on the wall of Ern McQuillan's Newtown gym. He allowed Dapra to throw punches non-stop until he finally tired of leniency and let the youngster have it, both barrels, right-left. Shingaki showed mere glimpses of his best, but his overall form convinced Fenech supporters to reach for some betting money.

Shingaki liked to dominate his opponents with his right hand lead, doubling and tripling up with his southpaw jab. Unlike most conventional left-handed fighters, he often fired a sharp right hook as the first punch of a combination and he could use both hands well when shooting for the body. His dangerous left cross was considered his chief weapon for the war that would take place just 24 hours after Anzac Day, 1985.

Shingaki showed something else too, a defence that leaked

punches, strength that would not stand up against Fenech's, and a distinct, almost suicidal, lack of confidence. He and his handlers had studied video tapes of Fenech's fights against Mulholland and Navarro, and while quick to praise Fenech's strength and durability, they predicted, probably without any real conviction, that the challenger would fall in eight. Fenech had other ideas and so did Lewis, who confessed the Japanese was maybe the weakest world champion in the sport's long, cruel history.

Fenech called John Lewis his secret weapon, convinced the three-and-a-half years he'd spent learning boxing from the Erskineville signwriter was more than enough to handle a champion whose record was decidedly underwhelming.

"John has me so fit there's no way my stamina will let me down," Fenech said, during the countdown. "Even when I was an amateur I trained as professionals do and I've sparred a lot of southpaws for this fight. My best shots are right rips to the body and rights to the chin — just the sort of thing for the Jap. I'll fight a smart fight. Keep the pressure on and wait to throw the right over the top."

Ever loyal to the man most responsible for his success, Fenech was also quick to point out that if ever he was going to win a world title, Shingaki was his best chance. Even though Lewis said he would accept full responsibility if Fenech lost, the fighter insisted he was not being rushed or overmatched.

"Blokes in the street are saying Lewie has put me in over my head," the challenger told reporters on the eve of the fight, "but I'd fight this bloke for nothing for the opportunity. Johnny has me so strong that I'll walk right through Shingaki. And, anyway, he hasn't had too many fights either. Why should I have to wait any longer? The people who arranged this, who agreed to the fight, obviously think I'm ready. I know I am. So let's get on with it."

Shingaki's nervous twitch would haunt him when he was asked to pose with Fenech at the Newtown Police Youth Club. Shingaki had the appearance of a lost puppy when Fenech, brimming with the same manufactured malice the Anzacs called on to discipline and motivate themselves against the enemy, strode across the boxing ring to shake hands. Shingaki smiled, a weak, nervous smile, blinked a few dozen times and wished he was somewhere else. He was wishing a lot more than that on April 26.

All along he had predicted he would be too tough and clever for the likes of a street brawler with a good manager. But Shingaki was soon exposed as a peaceful young man, who had no place in the uncompromising world of professional boxing. The Hordern Pavilion was throbbing with excitement on fight night. Channel 9 was telecasting the event live throughout the country, the first national telecast of an Australian fight since the fiasco between world-rated Paul Ferreri and long-retired veteran Rocky Gattellari six years earlier. That fight had featured the long-serving Australian champion, Ferreri, against an opponent who had fought for the world flyweight title in the mid-'60s and hadn't put on a boxing glove for years. It was a farce and set the sport back years with an Australian public becoming increasingly disinterested in broken noses and reeling senses. Ironically that fight was also held at the Hordern Pavilion. Now Fenech had the chance to rescue boxing from its shame.

Ferreri, the Melbourne veteran who was the first man to extend the great Mexican idol Carlos Zarate beyond 10 rounds, some nine years before, had demanded to fight Shingaki before Fenech. After all, here was a professional novice being granted a bantamweight title shot when Ferreri, who held both the Australian and Commonwealth bantamweight titles, wasn't even getting a look-in. Fenech was showing everyone the value of good management.

In Melbourne, Channel 7 was also televising the IBF junior lightweight title fight between Lester Ellis and the powerful-punching Rod Sequenan. Australia had staged just two world title fights since Johnny Famechon beat Fighting Harada at Sydney Stadium in 1969. The Stadium was demolished to make way for the Eastern Suburbs rail line and with its passing, the last rites were also administered to boxing in Australia. Now there were two world title fights on one night and all the attention was centered on Fenech. The Shingaki fight would outrate the much-watched television awards night, the Logies, the first time television's elite had ever been upstaged.

Green and gold balloons hovered above the ring, ready for the big occasion. There was a marching band and the biggest array of fight fans, crooks, colourful racing identities, sports stars and ex-pugs seen in Sydney for years. They were all there for one reason. One day after Anzac Day, the memories of World War II had conveniently come back to ensure a full house and five thousand voices to cheer on the local hero.

Shingaki's role as the villain in the Jeff Fenech story was

further exaggerated when he failed to appear in the championship ring on cue. Being the titleholder, he was rightfully entitled to enter the spotlight after the challenger. The champion's entrance is almost always the focal point of a title fight. Almost always, but not this time. There was only one star of this show. Shingaki would start the fight as a 10-9 betting favourite and at least one racing figure was said to have wagered $30,000 on the champion retaining his crown. One television reporter shook hands with Fenech and told the youngster he knew he could take the Jap's title. Then he left the dressing room and laid $300 on a Shingaki win.

IBF official Bill Brennan had described Shingaki as not being as strong as WBA and WBC champions Richie Sandoval and Albert Davila, but still "a talented world-class boxer". A lot of betting money was at stake. Only a sponsor was missing. The tobacco company Amatil had pulled out of the deal, along with its $100,000, because of the Australian Broadcasting Tribunal's tough stand on cigarette advertising. Still there were 5000 bums on seats and all involved in the financial side of the bout seemed happy enough.

Ray Connelly, the tuxedoed announcer with a semi-circle of grey hair and his thesaurus of introductions, told the crowd Shingaki was letting it be known he was champion and would come to the ring when he was ready. Maybe it was gamesmanship, maybe second thoughts or maybe another nervous trip to the toilet. In fact, Shingaki knew nothing about the delay. Promoter Bill Mordey had told Connelly to make the announcement, simply to whip up some more anti-Japanese feeling among the crowd. Fenech was seething. Finally Shingaki trotted through the crowd, the white-clad Mr Ikeda brandishing a gilded fist in an entrance that was barely a whimper compared to the wave of excitement generated by the appearance of Fenech and his handlers.

Shingaki was wearing a black and gold robe, red shorts and blue boots. Fenech, in a show of crowd-pleasing patriotism, was decked in green and gold robe with a boxing koala motif on the back. The crowd loved it.

Immediately the dissimilarities were apparent. Fenech, thin of leg, but broad of back and shoulder, was monstrous compared to the pale and seemingly under-nourished Japanese. He stalked the ring with all the hostility of a caged beast goaded by an electric prod, while Shingaki looked very much the reluctant warrior. His mind was elsewhere. James

Stevenson, the IBF vice-president and a man who had visited Australia three decades before as an adviser to world light-middleweight champion Ralph Dupas, shook hands with both boxers. Fenech hardly seemed to notice him. Shingaki smiled, blinked and seemed to be looking around for help. He was twitching again.

If the Australian public was expecting plenty of bloodletting, the Japanese would ensure it would be done with protocol and tradition. Fenech had many minutes to fan his inner fire. As the Japanese and Australian officials exchanged stuffed toy koalas and delicate Japanese dolls, the young challenger paced around the ring, throwing short fast punches into the air and occasionally nestling his head into Lewis' chest.

As perhaps the worst ever version of Advance Australia Fair droned around the hall, Fenech began fixing his blank stare, the kid of sociopathic facial vacuum that tells a victim there is no escape. The execution would be painful. No survivors. No prisoners.

As the anthem mercifully fades, Fenech begins high-stepping around his corner, arms waving above his head, the victory certain in his mind.

"Ladies and gentlemen," Connelly says as precise as a five-punch combination in which every blow hits the target, "Classic Promotions is proud to present a 15-round contest for the IBF .. ." ■

12
A Time For Hatred

"I hated my opponents. This was no passing dislike but a blazing virulent, powerful and consuming hatred. I believed I could not win without hatred, and win I must — because I was afraid to lose. Tragically, this hate, this fear became the fuel of my obsession to win"
Maureen Connolly,
tennis star, 1957.

In a gesture of respect that warriors seem to reserve for each other, Jeff Fenech brushed through the celebrating traffic jam to hoist the wobbly frame of Satoshi Shingaki shoulder high. Suddenly, as Australia's newest world boxing champion, he was embracing an adversary he had tried so hard to hate during the week of smouldering tension leading up to their fight.

This was the night of April 26, 1985, only 24 hours after television sets around Australia showed some of the surviving Anzacs and Turks, who had tried so hard to kill each other 70 years before, falling into each others' arms at a moving re-union where it all happened and where grains of sand were white again and not red with the blood of their comrades. These old fighting men had that special respect, too.

And once the battle was over in the Hordern Pavilion on that Friday night, so was Fenech's contrived malice towards a noble opponent he didn't even know — a slender, impeccably-groomed, polite young man. Shingaki was still on his feet when referee Bruce McTavish stepped in to save him from needless further punishment. And Fenech wanted to be the first to acknowledge his victim's courage. That was their first real contact without the gloves, the vivid yellow, eight-ounce gloves that had been carefully inspected and sealed in a box some 48 hours before the flurries were due to start.

Fenech had done his best to hate Shingaki before and during their fight. "I don't want anything to do with him," he kept muttering. "He might be a real nice bloke for all I know. But the last thing I want to do now is to start liking him. There's plenty of time for that after I take the title off him. Right now, I'm supposed to hate him. He's got what I want more than anything else in the world."

When it all happened at the Hordern Pavilion on that wet Friday night, Fenech's spontaneous reaction to the wonder of it all, might have had Sylvester Stallone accused of over-acting. As soon as a mercifully compassionate McTavish stepped in to call off the invasion of an already devastated target and pointed to Fenech as the new world champion, the swarthy, taut-framed kid flopped backwards to the canvas, exulting with outstretched gloves, as if his prayers had been answered by someone among the glare of lights high above. Anyone who might have flicked on the Nine Network's telecast of the fight at that very moment would have been totally misled; Shingaki still so gallantly upright and Fenech flat on his back. But only a matter of seconds later, Fenech was in the embrace of Johnny Lewis, who had vaulted through the ropes to savour the moment they had longed for, but never dared to take for granted.

For more than three years they had been working together in a relationship closer to father-and-son than trainer-and-fighter. More than three years of sweat and sacrifice that so often kept Lewis away from his wife and two young children and deprived Fenech of the simple pleasures most young men seem to take for granted. Every day they would be in the gym at the Newtown Police Youth Club, Lewis enforcing the physical and technical discipline and Fenech responding so uncomplainingly that the trainer knew almost from the start he was grooming a character of extraordinary commitment. As they seemed to disappear beneath a swarm of relatives and close friends who had simulated Lewis's invasion of the ring to acclaim them, all the striving had been worthwhile. The euphoria of strapping the glistening, gaudy, almost garish belt around his waist and responding to the crowd's roars of approval with the traditional salute, both arms raised high, must have been overwhelming.

But Fenech did not forget about the young man he had battered so relentlessly for nine rounds. It hadn't really been a close fight, but Shingaki still lost with honour, even by the lofty standards his country has traditionally demanded. He had proved himself a technically stylish boxer and as game as any who had stepped into an Australian ring in a long time. But it wasn't enough.

After a docile opening round that conformed with the traditional feeling-out period of such an important fight, Fenech ripped into action. It was clear the Australian had convinced himself, even at such an early stage, that the champion could not really hurt him. Apart from a fairly even sixth round, more through Fenech taking a breather than Shingaki launching a counter-attack, the betting men at ringside reflected smug contentment or grim resignation, depending on the direction they took in pre-fight transactions. Long before the end, most of Shingaki's backers were fumbling for their wallets to settle up. Only one result was possible.

It came after Fenech had punished his steadily-wilting target severely in rounds seven and eight, particularly with a stinging right hand that either snapped Shingaki's head back or smacked into his midriff loudly enough to be heard 20 rows back from the ring apron. Only 20 seconds from the end of round nine, two more spearing rights to Shingaki's jaw convinced McTavish that the brave Japanese champion wasn't going anywhere but down. If anything Shingaki's befuddled brain was at the gates of Disneyland instead of centre stage of the Hordern Pavilion. After stepping between Shingaki and any more punishment at two minutes and 32 seconds of the ninth, the referee made no apologies for a decision many, including the disconsolate Japanese camp, may have thought to be premature. "His brain was gone," McTavish insisted. "Only his fitness was keeping him up. You could see it in his eyes."

Suddenly Fenech no longer hated Shingaki. "You have to give the guy credit," Fenech said after hugging the well-worn loser. "I threw everything at him and he still wouldn't go down. He was like a kamikaze pilot. He just kept coming back at me. The last right I hit him with would have knocked out anyone, but he hung in there."

Shingaki would later protest the outcome. He said he'd been pacing himself and waiting for Fenech to tire. He said he's never really been hurt and deserved another try.

Fenech earned $20,000 for beating Shingaki and would later receive almost $100,00 for stopping him after three rounds in an August return bout. The inadequate Japanese was proving an easy source of revenue.

But on the night of April 26 money was the last thing on Jeff Fenech's mind. Among his family and friends there was a sense of fulfilment no winner's purse could buy. The street brawler had "done good". He'd taken something barbaric and made it, for the time being at least, more than acceptable. Enjoyable, watchable. He'd also made himself a celebrity.

In a winner's dressing room bulging with kissing relatives and back-slapping friends, the flash bulbs popped and television cameras whirred, and Jeff Fenech started thanking a list of people longer than the rolling credits on the Rocky films.

He dedicated his victory to Lewis, to Joe Fenech, the friend who had been electrocuted in a tragic work accident only a month or so before, and to Tania Foster, the girlfriend who had been at his side for so many of the troubled years until their tempestuous relationship died not long before the title fight only to be resurrected again and again.

When he mentioned her name, Fenech's voice broke just enough to betray how much he regretted her absence from ringside, where most loved ones are supposed to be on such occasions and where he had reserved a seat for her, just in case. He glanced across a few times between rounds, but it was empty. The din of a winning dressing room quickly jolted the new champion from any melancholy thoughts. Colin Love was there, his face reflecting relief, as much as joy. Con Spyropoulos was there, too. Con wasn't forgotten in his idol's greatest hour. As he ambled into the ring after the fight was stopped, Con was greeted by a bear-hug from the champ, and they paraded for several minutes, Fenech holding up Con's arm, as if he had done all the work. For nearly an hour, the Fenech dressing room was cramped. Many should never have been there but, then, championship boxing always attracts more than its share of fickle back-slappers, only interested in winners.

Limelighters who might have cynically sniggered at Fenech's world title hopes only a few months before, were there in droves, shouting to anyone who would listen that they always knew he could do it. Limelighters who weren't around when the hard climb was on, but were only too happy to accept the helicopter ride to enjoy the view from the top. Fenech knew they shouldn't have been there, but he couldn't have cared less. Because the people who really counted were there, too. People who had played salient parts in the remarkable story of Jeff Fenech.

He has never looked back since that night, which also salved his deepest wound — his elimination from the 1984 Olympic tournament. He vowed he would win a world title for Australia, little realising he would achieve it in only his seventh fight and after just 196 days as a pro. Success has never come faster for any boxer, anywhere in the world. It took Jimmy Carruthers 15 fights to claim Vic Toweel's world bantamweight title in '52 and everyone thought that was remarkable.

Fenech became the eighth Australian to claim a world championship. Les Darcy, who died in his prime in 1917, was widely regarded as a world middleweight champion, although some dispute his claim. Albert Griffiths (Young Griffo), held a disputed world featherweight title in the 1890s.

They preceded the Australian world champions of the modern era — Carruthers, Lionel Rose, Johnny Famechon, Rocky Mattioli and Lester Ellis, who successfully defended his IBF crown at Melbourne's Fesitval Hall against Sequenan only a few hours after the Marrickville kid had joined the select club.

Although he rarely drinks alcohol, the events that followed the spectacular night after Anzac Day were a soothing blur for Sydney's Rocky.

But as he embraced Satoshi Shingaki he didn't forget to pay his respects to the champion he had to beat to make it all possible. A brave warrior he no longer had to hate. ■

13
Poor Little Rich Boy

*"Interviewer: Have you ever been in love?
Muhammad Ali: Not with nobody else"*

The months immediately after Fenech's pummelling of Shingaki should have been the happiest of his young life.

He had, in the matter of months, weeks even, transformed himself through that frightening, yet somehow appealing, kind of brutality, from a $1,500-a-night club fighter into a $150,000-a-fight showpiece of Australian boxing.

Suddenly the paper boys and the politicians began to recognise him. Everywhere he went, a whole new wave of fans would try to drown him. Traffic would sometimes come to a halt when he'd take his car out in the daylight.

Shopkeepers and salesmen, publicists and profiteers gave him everything for nothing.

Suddenly, whatever he wanted was his — houses, cars, women, fame and adoration. At last, he was getting the spoils of a childhood spent trying to be bigger, stronger and tougher than kids twice his size.

Just before he had left Sydney for what would become the greatest adventure and the most painful disappointment of his career, Fenech's close friends and family gave him a going-away party to wish him well in his dream to become Australia's first Olympic gold medallist.

John Lewis had been there with some other close friends loyal to the cause. Fenech's sister Veronica cooked some calamari and prawns at the Marrickville unit, posters of Sylvester Stallone plastered on the walls and the Vietnamese people were arguing next door. Everyone had a good time.

Only a few months later at the 21st birthday of the world bantamweight champion, 70 people toasted his coming of age at an expensive beachside restaurant. Fenech's sponsor George Savvas, picked up the tab while Carlton and United

Breweries gave the champ a $100,000 sponsorship cheque as its much-publicised birthday present.

Lewis had enjoyed the Olympic farewell party a whole lot more.

After Fenech had savaged Shingaki, the relationship between fighter and father-figure had become so strained that it was in grave danger of being irreparably rent. Eventually Lewis, Fenech's finder, mentor and friend, told the champion and monster he created that he'd had enough. After all the hurt they'd endured together and all the joys they had shared, Lewis told Fenech to get out of his home, to stay out of his gym and to keep out of his life.

"They were bad times," Lewis recalls, relieved that they are no more and careful to see them banished for good. "In the end I'd just had a gutful of Jeff acting like a lair. And I told him so. At that time he was forever confusing the fairweather friends he'd inherited with the genuine mates who'd helped him when he was nothing. He was starting to run with the new crowd. Suddenly, the fair dinkum friends were no longer good enough.

"There was a great deal of tension between us. Now that he'd become the champ he felt no one had the right to tell him how to live. No one but Jeff could decide right from wrong. I tried to talk to him about it but he'd become so stubborn it was like talking to a brick wall. In the end I honestly felt we'd both be a lot happier if we went our separate ways. I believed I'd be happier if he went and trained with someone else. I knew he wouldn't have to look far for someone to put him through punches."

One of Australian sport's most successful partnerships was on the way out. It had been a long time coming.

Fenech is an ingratiating character who can be as appealing and as charming as royalty. All his life he grew up discovering the world and its ways for himself, learning an intricate kind of street psychology, instinctively knowing the right things to say and just how to say them.

To his friends Fenech is one of the beautiful people: generous, funny, considerate and fiercely loyal. He can be one of those loveable rogues who makes you feel good just by being around. But no one, not even the most cunning and self-assured slum boy, can walk off the back alley and into easy street without teething troubles.

For the boxer whose whole life hovers between diet and dehydration, pain and pounding, the roads from austerity are broken by gaping pitfalls. For a kid who always wanted to be a star, who craved to be the object of idolatory ever since he'd first picked up a football, the headlines and platitudes became bigger dangers than facing a pair of sluggers with iron chins and steel hearts.

As he became more accusomted to the interview, the photograph and the quick TV grab, he became more extroverted. The humility started peeling off him like skin from a snake. He told Ita Buttrose the girl he'd like to marry would have to be pretty dumb because he liked the idea of being able to play up without getting caught. Before his predictably one-sided slashing of Shingaki in their August return fight, he spoke of the way he planned to torture the shy Japanese; how he wanted to hurt him real bad for daring to under-rate the severity of the first beating.

"I want him to feel all the pain," Fenech would taunt at every opportunity. "I want to bust him up. Of course, I could bash him in one round if I really wanted to, but I'm going to let it go the full 15. I'll make every round agony for him."

By the time of the return fight, Fenech was taking great delight in admitting his almost homicidal hatred for opponents. It wasn't so much the kind of supernatural fitness Lewis and he had produced in something like 5000 hours together inside the Newtown gym over three-and-a-half years, nor the rapidly developing boxing skills that had made Fenech so successful so soon. It was a burning, callous contempt for anyone who got in his way and a total disregard for their well-being that opened the gates to easy street.

It was the same kind of contempt that made Roberto Duran, the Panama City gutter child, the greatest lightweight fighter of all time. Although Fenech never had it anywhere near as tough as the demonic slugger they called Hands of Stone — Duran grew up fighting other street waifs for food— he developed a similar pathological disdain for anyone who opposed him.

Before every important fight he developed a self-induced catatonic state where all his jovial banter and hyperactivity were driven away by a stone-faced malevolence. He closed his mouth tighter than Sugar Ray Robinson's defence. He just sat in his dressingroom, legs twitching, jaw bones grinding together. As though to release a single murmur would sap some of that fine tuned strength. And ever since he labelled poor little Bobby Williams a "little XXXX" before his professional debut at the end of '84, each opponent would die a thousand deaths inside Fenech's mind.

It was only when the same mentality began to encroach on life outside the ring that Lewis became intolerant. When the anomalies became paramount. When Fenech would be so exciting in the boxing ring and yet such an insufferable bore when the fighting was done. The trainer became incensed when Fenech would start to treat friends like flunkies, ignoring the mates who counted for the ones craving a share of the limelight. When he would get trusted pals to carry his ice cream like pageboys and when he tried to make the people who loved him become his stooges. When the stories of fights in discos and an unrepentant attitude forced Fenech into a showdown at Lewis' modest lounge room.

It wasn't the first time Lewis had been confronted by his fighter's rage nor is it likely to be the last. Ever since he'd watched as his budding champ distorted the face of a bigger kid after his first amateur fight, Lewis has been a constant safety valve for Fenech's temper.

Sometimes he'd get the call to calm the fighter down when he threatened to smash up the furniture because a girlfriend wasn't home when he called. Sometimes he'd have to talk to the local police and plead that they have mercy on a good kid with some bad inclinations.

Fenech remembers their living room showdown with a tinge of sadness, wishing it had never happened. For a while he had even prepared to quit boxing, get out with the money he'd already made and try and make a name for himself in his first great passion, rugby league.

If the taxmen hadn't been so inconsiderate he might well have retired after the shortest, most spectacular career of any world champion.

"Before I won the world title Lewie and me never had an argument, hardly even a cross word. Suddenly with so many opportunities to have some laughs, but with everyone watching me and feeding him with stories, we were bickering all the time. Blokes would pick fights with me to prove how tough they were. I knew as soon as I hit them it would be all over the front pages and I'd be in the shit again with John. For a long time I thought about quitting boxing so I could be John's friend without the hassles."

Lewis, instead, decided to opt out of their working relation-

Fenech found an able training "partner" in the lead-up to his fight with Jerome Coffee — John Lewis's son Brent. Photo Michael Amendolia, The Daily Telegraph

Above: Steve McCrory took a terrible beating in Olympic Revenge. But in the sixth round, he stung a weakened Fenech with his best blows.

Right: Even though he was starved and sore, Fenech still had the strength to overpower McCrory and win by knockout. Photo: Peter Solness.

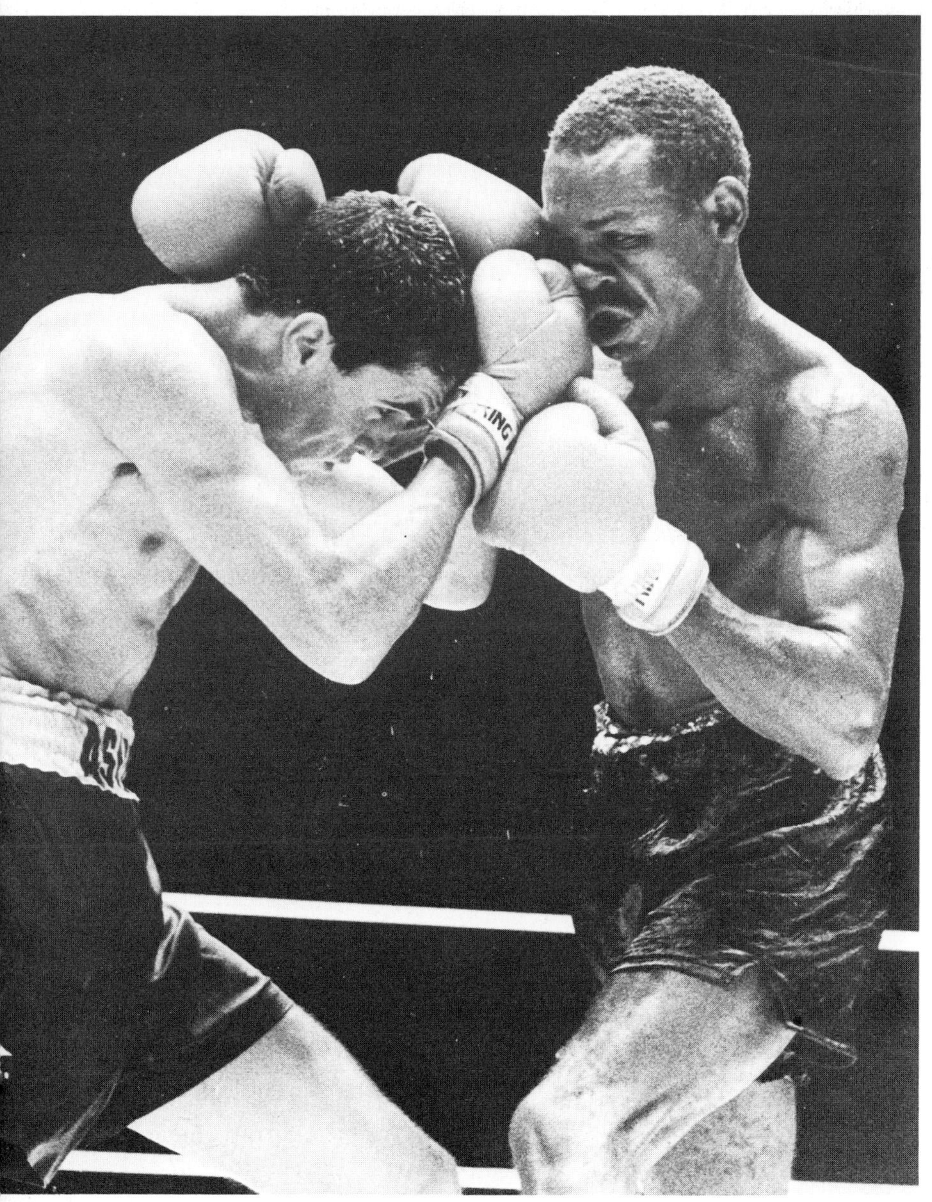

*Jerome Coffee had a big mouth
before the fight. After it, his nose
had also been spread a little wider.
Photo Vic Sumner. John Fairfax & Sons.*

Above: Fenech's retarded
mate Con has helped the
champion as much as the
champion has helped him.

Right: Fenech became
Australia's real life Rocky.
Photo: Paul Johns.
The Daily Mirror.

ship. Fenech could still be a mate but only if he went and trained somewhere else. When, finally, he told the champ to go looking for another trainer, he was prepared for a calamitous confrontation.

"Instead Jeff broke down in tears, stormed out of my place and shouted back to me that it was all over," Lewis remembers. Within five minutes the world champion was on the phone using the little boy voice he sometimes employs when he wants something badly. "He said 'Johnny, I'm sorry. I never wanted it to go this far. I never wanted to be bad friends'.

"I told him it was too late to apologise," Lewis said, "That I couldn't be bothered wasting my time on a big head anymore. Jeff swore at me and hung up and may God strike me dead I thought that would be the last we'd ever speak. I started to feel sad all over and just as I began thinking about all the great times we had together there he is in front of me smiling the same way he does in a photo of us together on my living room wall. We've had a few rough times since, but Jeff is the kind of kid who hates letting his friends down."

Fenech went back to Lewis because a career without the man who taught him how to fight and devised the tactics to make him a success, would be no career at all.

"I decided a long time ago," Fenech said, "When it first looked like I could make a bit of a name for myself in boxing that Johnny would be the only trainer I'd ever have. That's what used to piss me off so much about the amateurs. I'd go to places all over the world. To America where all the trainers were supposed to be so shit hot and Lewie knew more about how to train a boxer and how to bring out the best qualities in him than just about all the other trainers I saw put together. God forbid, if anything ever happened to him and he couldn't train me anymore, I'd have to give boxing away no matter how much money they offered me."

Despite the bonds which grew back even stronger after their verbal brawl, there have been many tensions since.

In Brisbane in November, 1985, on the day he was due to fight the comic Kenny Butts, Fenech showed once again, irrefutably, that life as an instant celebrity, despite its tempting trappings, could be worse than living on the streets. A few hours before what was supposed to be a warm-up for the imminent title defence against America's Jerome Coffee, Fenech had gone on an emotional rampage inside his hotel suite.

Lewis had put the torch to Fenech's inflammable ego, remonstrating with him over the manner in which he was handling his new superstar status. Fenech didn't like the truth. Now Lewis was trying to soothe the beastial fury of a boxer with bruised pride. But Fenech would have none of it. He stalked around his room cursing and snarling, kicking over a pot plant, putting his feet through a lamp, tossing tables at the wall. He rammed his shoulder against a solid timber door hoping it would shatter like matchstick. A little grey-haired maid whose commonsense was better than her English scurried for cover in another room.

"Everyone can get——," he bellowed with such volume that the hotel security guards came running. "Youse 'ave all brushed me. No one'll talk to me. I'm sick of fightin' anyway. Tell Mordey to get me on the first plane back to Sydney. I'm not fightin' nobody."

His body shook all over as though some mind-disturbing fever had gripped him in delirium. Twice Fenech shaped to explode his right fist, the same fist which so befuddled the brains of Shingaki and a dozen other rivals, through his distorted reflection in a plate glass window. But even with tears pouring down his brown face and the curses pouring from his mouth, he still had enough street cunning left to realise a handful of stitches was bad for business.

"C'mon, Jeff, I didn't want it to come to this," Lewis begged, throwing an arm around the fighter's waist, "Let's sit down and have a talk. We can work things out. We always have."

But with the migrant maid cowering in another room Fenech stalked off to pack his bag. Lewis shrugged and went to lie by the hotel swimming pool. If his champion didn't feel like fighting there wasn't much he could do about it.

A few hours later with no one really sure whether there was going to be a boxing match or not, Fenech phoned Lewis' room and as if nothing had happened between them that afternoon, asked what time they'd be walking down to the House of Stoush, Festival Hall.

That night, after Peter Mitrevski had won a preliminary bout and the old Olympic mate Shane Knox had made a knockout professional debut, the Marrickville Mauler won the most absurd fight he's ever likely to have.

Kenny Butts came to Brisbane after extending Olympic champ Steve McCrory the full distance in an eight-round bout that suggested the gold medallist would not be the same force in the paid ranks that he had been as a world amateur champion.

Butts, about the same height as circus clown Bobby Williams, but much shorter on gumption, had a record of 10 wins and two draws in 15 fights and was based at the same gym as another occasional visitor to Australia, Charlie "Choo Choo" Brown, a former world lightweight champion. Not much was known about Butts, but the speculation was rife. One journalist went so far as to describe him as "rugged" in the lead-up to the non-title fight. Or rather non-title bout, since the only fighting came when disgusted ringsiders demanded their money back.

Originally Fenech was supposed to fight his old amateur enemy Tony Miller, but for the second time the Melbourne boxer declined to try to even the score. Butts came in as a last-minute substitute. He was paid $6000 and given a holiday in sunny Queensland. For the lack of effort he produced and allowing for even a smattering of decency on his part, Butts should have given promoter Mordey an instant cash refund.

Taking the lift to the pre-fight weigh-in, Butts and his trainer, Arnold Mitchell laughingly recalled the time they'd been in an elevator in New Mexico when the cable snapped and they crashed a few floors in an express ride to the lobby. Any notion Butts had of giving Fenech a hard night's work came crashing down as soon as he stared straight ahead and found Fenech's sternum.

For two rounds the Philadelphia experiment who was proud of coming from the same city as the most revered of hard men, Joe Frazier and Bennie Briscoe, ran backwards, jumped behind the referee, ducked down to the level of Fenech's knees and generally made himself scarcer than a farmyard turkey at Christmas time.

In the second round it sounded like one of the few blows Fenech had managed to tag on the tearaway target might have broken Butt's jaw. It hadn't, but Butt's butt had been kicked enough. He wasn't coming out for round three. Predictably the crowd, cheated of a good night's violence, booed.

Fenech, time wasted, hotel suite wasted, but his stamina and strength totally conserved, flew home to Sydney next morning. Though he had achieved nothing tangible from two rounds of chasing an ever-retreating shadow, he had learned something important from the experience.

"The day Jeff blew up before the Butts fight was the last time he really gave me any cause for concern," Lewis said, "Once we had our differences out in the open and he started to see things my way, he started to realise that a little moderation in life was necessary. His attitude became more professional and mature. I think he started getting his priorities right about that time."

The Kenny Butts bout was Fenech's second in the Queensland capital and the contrast between bemusing Butts and Fenech's first Brisbane victim, the resolute Briton John Farrell, was immense.

Farrell was the second best bantamweight in England and had drawn with the champion Ray Gilbody. He was a gritty little bruiser in the tradition of the British bulldog and his refusal to give in against Fenech typified the harsh environment in which his fighting instincts had been nurtured in Kirby, Lancashire. There he was something of a working class hero. Farrell was a 27-year-old southpaw with a wife, a kid, 10 wins and a draw in 12 fights and plenty of "bottle" — he had the heart to go with his overflow of self-confidence.

Fenech and Farrell fought in July, 1985, a month before Fenech fought the return with Shingaki and four months before the comedy, starring Kenny Butts. Farrell gave Fenech a far tougher test than Shingaki could have mounted even if he'd been allowed to carry that sumarai sword into the ring. Farrell brought out the best and the worst in the bantamweight champion, the animalistic ferocity that drives him to success.

Paul and Mary Fenech rode the train to Brisbane to watch the Farrell fight using their pensioner concession cards. By the time Kenny Butts came along Fenech could afford to pay for his father's first nervous jet flight.

Farrell and Shingaki, whose style the Englishman was supposed to emulate, had little in common except they both jabbed with their right hand, both were knocked out by Fenech in the ninth round and both had a hazardous overabundance of courage. But while Shingaki looked ashenly apprehensive, Farrell approached the meeting with self-assuredness.

At the weigh-in half a day before he'd endure all kinds of torment, Farrell turned up in a double-breasted suit and a cheeky grin. He undressed while waving to women in the crowd and told everyone they were in for a big surprise when it came time to fight.

But if it seemed he was suffering from a swollen head before the fight, that was nothing compared to the way his face ballooned in nine rounds with Fenech. After a half hour of hell, Farrell's face was red and black and blue. His lips had been scraped raw, his eyes swollen shut, his cheek bones covered in bruises and his ribs in a cluster of welts from Fenech's rattatatt body attack. He put the Savil Row suit on again the next day, but he needed sunglasses to go with it.

Fenech's ninth knockout in nine fights not only ended Farrell's dream of forcing a title bout with the IBF champion, but it also ended the personal agony of Lewis. Brisbane had been a bad scene. Not only had Lewis suffered nausea and heart palpatations from what was diagnosed as extreme nervousness leading up to the bout and throughout the nine rounds it lasted, but he'd also been badly bruised and lamed after becoming a casualty in Australia's modern day Civil War — the rugby league State of Origin match between New South Wales and Queensland at Lang Park.

Thirty thousand Queenslanders gathered there to drink a lot, swear a lot and boo the Blues. The Queensland-NSW rugby league matches are the pillars of parochialism and probably the best method Brisbane has to induce mass hysteria outside of threatening the state with a Liberal Government.

When one stumbling Queensland supporter speared Lewis onto a concrete path outside the ground, he had no idea he'd just belted the man behind the best known fighter in Australia. Fenech and another of Lewis' trained "assassins", middleweight Hit Man Jeff Harding were standing nearby. They were in no mood to take prisoners. For a few seconds, they used that unknowing league fan as a cross between a heavy punching bag and a giant sized football, and if Lewis hadn't recovered enough to drag them away, it's unlikely the hapless Queenslander would ever have tasted Fourex again.

A few days later, Farrell was the victim in a $200,000 tournament sponsored by the Tooheys brewery and designed to showcase, through national television, the talents of Australian boxing's latest hero. The first fight in the tournament had been against an out-toughed Filipino featherweight John Matienza who flew into Sydney with a record of 18 wins in 19 fights and a head cold later aggravated by a few cracked ribs sustained in six trying rounds and three trips to the canvas.

Matienza was the first opponent in a blueprint to turn Fenech into a world champion of far greater ability than half a dozen fights would seem to justify.

"People still don't realise that when Jeff won the world title he was a total novice," Lewis said, "If I wasn't certain he could beat Shingaki, I would never have taken the title fight. But once he won the championship it was like suddenly being thrown into the deep end of a swimming pool.

"Coffee was waiting to win the title and we had to stall him as long as we could. I had to get Jeff fights against all kinds of opponents with a whole variety of styles, I had to help him develop a maturity inside the ring and out. I had to change him from a rookie into an experienced and capable world champion. I guess in the long run I had to change him from being a boy into being a man."

With his own head cold and an infected ear which became the target for Matienza's left hooks, Fenech had to be content with seeing the Filipino twice climb off the canvas before all the fight was knocked out of him. Every time Matienza landed one of his left hooks it was like someone had hit Fenech in the head with a hammer. But he didn't mind so much. It just meant he'd have to hurt Shingaki just a little bit more.

The most stunning aspect about the Fenech-Shingaki rematch was that so many people actually believed the International Boxing Federation was coming down hard on the little Aussie battler who claimed he was getting ripped off just like back in LA.

Shingaki, or rather the heartless schemers who pushed him back into the ring for a second nightmare, had demanded a rematch on the grounds that their over-matched fighter had been upright, even if ever so barely, when referee McTavish mercifully ended his suspect reign as a world champion.

Promoter Mordey, understandably, squeezed every bit of publicity he could from the IBF decision and there were all kinds of wailing headlines and tear-jerking television interviews lamenting the fate of poor little Jeff.

Of course Fenech was aware all along that the rematch was the best thing that could happen to him since he walked into the Police Boys Club looking for trouble in 1981. Instead of having to trade blows with the infinitely more experienced Coffee, Fenech would earn close enough to $100,000 for fighting Shingaki, an opponent who was out of the race before the starter's gun had gone off. And by fighting Shingaki a second time he was able to keep Coffee at bay for another four months.

Jay Edson, a roly-poly manager of a greyhound track in Arizona, was appointed to referee his 49th world title fight and to make sure there were no doubts about the outcome a second time. Channel 9 billed the bout "Return of the Ninja", but might just as well have suggested it as a first draft for "The Killing Fields".

Paul Fenech was there to see his son defend the world title which made them both so puffed with pride. There shouldn't have been anything extraordinary in Paul's presence except that two weeks before his son's first title defence, Paul and Jeff had said their goodbyes. The frail Maltese migrant prepared for another trip into the great beyond. Yet another of his brushes with death kept Fenech commuting between hospital and gymnasium. He'd tell his friends and family that even though his father might die he'd still give it to Shingaki. Whether Paul really wanted it like that, Fenech had come too far to stop now. Paul looked a little pale and drawn as he shuffled towards his ringside seat but he was there to cheer his faltering heart out.

Just about everyone in the auditorium, including Shingaki, knew it was no contest right from the start. They held the fight in the State Sports Centre at Homebush Bay, built on the site of an old slaughterhouse and by the time the world title fight ended after just nine minutes, Shingaki looked like he'd been hacked open with a boning knife.

There was blood everywhere. All over his sad face and all over Fenech's dry-cleaned white trunks and sun-tanned chest. Seconds after the start Fenech squashed Shingaki's nose and started the blood-letting. By the second, a flurry of big punches opened an inch-long cut by Shingaki's right eye. For the sake of bravado, something he was unashamedly big on at the time, Fenech claimed a head butt did all the damage. After the third and bloodiest round — a good one for the boxing abolitionists — Edson waved his hands to say no more.

Shingaki, showing there was no limit to his courage even if there was to his skills, shaped up to Edson like he was fit enough to fight both referee and world champion. But Edson only shook his head. "Look at your face, look at all the blood," he told Shingaki. "Your eye is horrible. It's too bad to fight anymore." Shingaki didn't speak English, but he got the message loud and clear.

Later the referee, who had controlled bouts featuring some of the greatest champions in history, explained his decision: "When a cut is so bad that you can see right down to the bone, you know it's time to call it quits. Shingaki was being out-punched. Even if it had gone on, Fenech was just too strong."

As soon as Edson crowned him the winner Fenech grabbed the microphone and told an internaional TV audience he re-gretted it was over so quickly because the cut eye had ruined the torture he had in mind. He'd wanted to bounce Shingaki off the floor a few times just to give him a few painful remind-ers of Australian hospitality. Somewhere Paul Hogan and tourism minister John Brown might have been cringing.

Lewis merely raised his eyes to the heavens and wondered when Fenech would ever grow up. But really he didn't have to wait too long.

When Jerome Coffee left Nashville to fulfil a lifetime am-bition the boy he expected to be waiting for him had vanished for good. In his place was a hardened professional, the ban-tamweight champion of the world and a 21-year-old no longer hell bent on destruction. Just winning. ∎

14
Fighting Clever

*"Float like a butterfly, sting like a bee; you
cannot hit what you cannot see."*
*Drew "Bundini" Brown,
Ali's cornerman, 1964.*

All around him there was darkness permeated only by the
far-off twinkling of a thousand flash bulbs. There was
silence too, an eerie, empty, hollow silence broken only by the
echoing murmurs of uncertainty. Silence and darkness like
an astronaut stranded in outer space. His only hope of
making the mission a success hinging on one good right hand.

Jerome Coffee's mind raced quickly, his logic trying to out-
pace the emotions flaring in his heart. He knew he was desperate, but he also knew that one good right hand could do
the job. One good right hand would let him stay unbeaten and
walk away with the only prize that ever mattered to him — a
world professional boxing title.

For fleeting moments Coffee was oblivious to the voices in
his ear. Early in the fight the sounds had been gentle and reassuring. The sounds of a mother teaching her baby to walk.
Now they were frantic and goading. The maddened cries of
revolutionaries at a public execution.

"Whip him good, he's yours, man," Stan Allen was imploring with all the urgency his southern drawl could muster.

"C'mon kid the title's yours. Take it. Right hands. Right
hands. He's shot."

Jerome "Kid" Coffee now listened to his manager like a
thief turning the tumblers of a safe. The more he listened the
more he liked what he heard. Sure Jeff Fenech was tired. If he
felt anything like the burn in his lungs and the numbness in
his arms that Coffee was experiencing, he had already entered the mirrored room of infinite exhaustion. That place of
baffling distortion and deceit where the target becomes a

miriad of painful images. That room where the lethargy and hurt are iron bars on the windows to escape.

But of course this weariness had been expected; indeed it had all been part of Coffee's fight plan. The swarthy little street fighter across the ring had been pushed past nine rounds for the first time in his life and there he was, a well-publicised novice, struggling through rounds 10 and 11. "Oh sure," Coffee reasoned, "The street brawler threw good shots early, threw me around a mite, but now he was ready for the whipping he deserved."

Rounds 10 and 11 had been two of Coffee's best in a fight Fenech was dominating. The flow was changing. For the first time in his professional career, perhaps in his whole boxing life, Fenech had really been hurt. He would never admit it, but a Coffee right had shaken him in the 10th, had made John Lewis' heart miss a beat and had sent gasps of anguish through Fenech's family sitting at ringside. It had also made the young champion's legs tremble and had seen him pinned against the ropes for frightening moments near the end of the round.

In the 11th, Coffee had made Fenech take more steps in retreat and for the first time since the deputy sheriff from Nashville had come out banging jabs to the head and body in the opening minutes of the fight, his supporters were thinking maybe, just maybe, he had enough firepower to storm home and take the title.

At ringside Barry Michael, the tough Melbourne veteran who had outpointed Lester Ellis for the IBF junior-lightweight title, was starting to show concern at the mettle of the unbeaten black American.

"Coffee is showing up better in these last two rounds," Michael told his audience, "I'm sure his corner is telling him that he's behind on points and that if he wants to take the title back to the USA he's got to do more."

Coffee's corner was doing just that. After 33 minutes of combat Jerome's time had arrived. His trainer Clint Jackson, who had come so close himself, only to fall in the big fights, was telling his man that the battle plan had reached its most critical stage.

"Now's the time," Jackson prodded, his black, broken nose twitching. "Right hands. Right hands."

"Right on," Coffee shouted back, his eyes wild with a vision of violent ecstacy. Among the tribes of Southern Africa they call such frenzied enthusiasm the "Divine Madness". Witch doctors have been known to drive whole tribes to genocide. In Hitler's Germany, they called it propaganda. In boxing, it's called one last shot.

"Right on," Coffee continued, his eyes flashing hate across the ring. Dark eyes that had once flashed cruelly when, like his adversary, he too had brushed roughly against the hardness of the law. Now Coffee's head swivelled around his giraffe's neck and his face of scorn came into direct gaze with Fenech's. The hated Fenech. Spite and contempt lashed from Coffee's face. Total disregard for the abilities of a rookie who didn't deserve the title. Hatred for a kid who got lucky and got to Shingaki first.

Fenech, eyes reddened by sweat and pain, stared back devoid of expression. Ever so slyly he poked out his tongue like a child who has something the other boy wants but isn't about to give it away. Jerome Coffee would never beat Jeff Fenech. Not in the 12th round, not ever. After all, the Marrickville Mauler had a point to prove.

Fenech first heard of Jerome Coffee in March, 1985. Not long before he'd scored his fifth straight knockout win by stopping Mulholland for the NSW bantamweight title. Now he was training for Rolly Navarro. A win over the Filipino would give him a title shot against Satoshi Shingaki. A win over Shingaki meant he would have to fight the unbeaten American who'd been around a long time but had failed to break into the really big time of pro boxing. No Las Vegas title fights, no national television extravaganzas. Coffee had been boxing for a decade and a half, but wasn't known much outside of Nashville, Tennessee, a place more famous for country music than world boxing champs.

Coffee had only been the No. 3 contender for Shingaki's world title, but since the two fighters rated above him, Texan Gaby Canizales and Korean Chan Yung Park, showed little interest in meeting the Japanese champion, Coffee was the organisation's "leading available challenger".

After four years of professional boxing in which he'd never been really hurt, his carefully planned route to the top was working. He'd never met a really dangerous opponent, and unbeaten and unscathed he'd found himself getting ready to fight an unknown Japanese for a version of the world bantamweight title.

His old foe Richie Sandoval had won the World Boxing Association title and now Coffee was just one easy fight away from joining his former amateur nemesis as joint ruler of the 118-pound division. Satoshi Shingaki, after all, would be easy pickings. Less difficult than most of those lillywhites he'd given boxing lessons to on the way to compiling 193 wins in 205 amateur bouts. Coffee knew it, Shingaki knew it, Jeff Fenech knew it and most importantly John Lewis knew it.

While Shingaki was doing his darndest to avoid fighting Coffee, who was running into so many detours, Lewis was already planning a short cut to steal the crown. He knew that somewhere along the line Fenech would have to fight Coffee but they could always cross that bridge when they came to it. He knew also that Fenech would stand a far greater chance of beating Coffee if he went into the bout as a more experienced champion than a less-experienced challenger. And in any case as world champion Fenech could stall Coffee for as long as he liked. Eventually eight months.

"When the time comes I know Jeff will be hot for Coffee," Lewis would say, not realising the pun. "He's improving so rapidly that it's only a matter of time before he's good enough for the fight. We're learning more and more about Coffee. He's been fighting pro for five years but so far hasn't created much of an impression. His best achievements were as an amateur, but that was a long time ago and a whole different ball game."

Indeed it had been a long time ago, but despite his outward enthusiasm, Lewis was still wary of a boxer who'd been honing his skills since before Fenech started school. From the time Fenech entered the ring with Shingaki on April 26 to the Coffee fight on December 2, he'd fought five times for a total of 29 rounds. Coffee had fought just twice in 18 months for a total of six rounds against mediocre opposition. He'd also been studied by Lewis the way a pathologist investigates a new and deadly virus. Every potentially useful piece of information was compiled as Coffee was examined in microscopic detail.

Coffee had his first amateur fight when he was 12. His love of the sport had started years before when he and his grandpa would watch Cassius Clay float like a butterfly and sting like a bee against a variety of opponents beginning with that Big Ugly Bear, Sonny Liston. Speed and skill against brawn and brute strength. Little Jerome's greatest wish was to be just like Cassius Clay.

He also wanted to be a gymnast: "I had the quickness. I had the guts. I had the natural ability. But where I grew up (in a part of Nashville the locals called "South Vietnam") the only gymnastics was hot-wiring cars and jumping over fences when the police sirens started."

South Vietnam's local sheriff, a man with the apt name of Fate Thomas and the nickname of Boss Hog, took an interest in the brash but likeable youngster with boundless energy and valuable athletic gifts.

"It's the boxing gym or jail," Thomas told the kid. Nine years later and with the sheriff's sponsorship, Jerome Coffee was the best amateur flyweight boxer in the world. He picked up some battle scars against the Czechs and the Cubans, but in 1979 he was the US amateur champion, favourite for the Olympic gold medal and part of a star national squad that included some of the finest professional talent of the 1980s.

There was the light-flyweight champion Sandoval, a Mexican-American who would narrowly outpoint Coffee in the flyweight final for a place at the Moscow Olympics, a place that would never be filled because of President Jimmy Carter's Olympic boycott. Sandoval would become WBA champion and, until he was put in a hospital bed by Gaby Canizales, was considered the best bantamweight in the world.

Also in the US squad of '79 were seven future world champions like Donald Curry, Mike McCallum and Coffee's Nashville team-mate Johnny Bumphus. There were others too, like Bernard Taylor and Joe Frazier's son, Marvis, who would become leading pro contenders.

Coffee was certainly from fine fighting stock. He'd beaten a dual Olympic gold medallist, Jose Hernandez of Cuba, and had developed a hit-and-run style perfect for amateur boxing and, in his heart, perfect for exposing the limitations of a strong but inexperienced street fighter.

"I've said my prayers, I've paid my dues and I'm polishing my tools," Coffee said over and over again in a variety of interviews before the Fenech fight. "I've been fighting for 15 years. I've earned a world title. Jeff Fee-neck has come along real easy. Now it's Coffee time"

Coffee had simmered inside for 12 months chasing Shingaki, trying to trap him inside a boxing ring. He boiled over when he heard Shingaki was taking a warm-up bout with Fenech. But when the IBF did the Australian a favour by granting Shingaki a return fight, Coffee was aglow with anger. Manager Stan Allen, a cautious and gracious attorney who, among other interests, represented Elvis Presley's step-mother and an Elvis lookalike in neighbouring Memphis, threatened the IBF with a million-dollar law suit if his fighter didn't get the opportunity he so rightly deserved. Back home, Lewis was getting Fenech ready for Shingaki II, but his mind was occupied more with a small black figure with fast hands and a faster mouth.

"Tell Mr Fee-neck I'm ready to rumble," Coffee said in telephone interviews from his apartment overlooking the Tennessee grass of a Nashville golf course.

"Hit and not be hit — that's my style. He who hits and runs away lives to hit another day. I'm a boxer, a mover, but I know I can take a man out if I catch him good. Mr Shingaki was nuthin'. Mr Fee-neck ain't much better."

Coffee was a promoter's dream. A former street hoodlum like Fee-neck, he now worked as a deputy sheriff for Boss Hog. He also spoke to youngsters on the folly of drug and alcohol abuse. The full circle. A part-time tailor, he made all his own tracksuits and boxing shorts (Fee-neck used to steal his) and he was trained by Clint Jackson, captain of the great 1976 US Olympic boxing team. The wife of Coffee's manager, a Southern belle, named Betty Sue Allen, worked the fighter's corner.

Further news began to filter through about Coffee's ability. In hot, humid Darwin, Barry Michael was preparing to successfuly defend his IBF junior-lightweight title for the first time against South Korean Jin Sik Choi and spent some of his time away from training, assessing the chances of his fellow Australian world title holder.

"I saw Jerome Coffee fight when I was in the States," Michael said, hours away from stopping Choi in four, "He's very slick and very fast, but you find a lot of these guys with great records have been nurtured along all their lives. When they strike someone who refuses to lose, they're found wanting. Coffee can move beautifully, but he's no great puncher and I'm certain that over 15 rounds Jeff will just wear him down and wear him out." ■

15
Coffee Time

"Man I am so fast that when I go to bed at night, I can switch off the light and be under the covers before it gets dark"

Muhammad Ali.

By the time Jerome Coffee arrived in Sydney for the fight with Fenech, he remained, to most, a mystery boxing figure. His manager, the quiet but quotable, Stan Allen, described him as being America's fastest boxer on his feet and third fastest with his hands, which certainly supported Barry Michael's opinion of him.

Others said Coffee was a bum. A carefully-protected, technically-perfect stylist, who would crumble as soon as he felt the hammers from a hardened professional. Coffee's name troubled some sections of media. Fenech may have been one of the best known identities in the country, but his opponents were still far from household names. Coffee was variously referred to as Jeremy Coffey, Jaramy Cofey, Jerome Cofey and even Jeremy Coney, who in fact was the New Zealand cricket skipper about to wreak his own havoc on the Australian sporting public.

By the time Coffee walked through the customs checks at Sydney Airport to be met by the blinding glare of flash bulbs and arc lights of the television cameras, some were saying he had the punching power of George Foreman, the speed of Sugar Ray Leonard, the strength of Joe Frazier and the mouth of Muhammad Ali.

They were right about the mouth.

Ghetto-blaster driving out the latest hits from Motown and his clicking fingers and dancing feet jiving to the beat, Coffee was certainly no inarticulate pug. He liked his reputation as a loquacious larruper. A man who could roll out the words faster than his stinging straight left.

"Like John Rambo I've come here with both guns in hand to get what's mine," Coffee announced at the airport press conference, holding up both his tiny fists for the scrutiny of intrigued media members.

"When the smoke clears and the dust settles on December 2, there'll only be one fighter left standing and it sure won't be Jeff Fee-neck. He's durable, he's young, aggressive and he's in big trouble.

"I hear there'll be 11,000 people cheering for him. But while the crowd might be his, the space inside those four posts is all mine."

Coffee even said he'd devised a special punch for the fight, a looping right hand he called "The Coffee Creamer". He'd rehearsed his lines well. Maybe he'd been rattling them off to the other members of his entourage all the way from Nashville. It would have helped to ease the tension for a veteran fighter with one good shot at stardom and a tough, strong kid in his way.

Coffee was the star of the Clint Jackson Punchin' Posse. Jackson was 31 years old and, a decade before, the leader of the finest Olympic team ever assembled. In 1976, his teammates Sugar Ray Leonard, Leon and Michael Spinks and Leo Randolph all won gold medals at Montreal and went on to win world professional titles. Big John Tate, a pensive giant from nearby Knoxville, Tennessee, was flattened in one round by Teo Stevenson, the three-time Olympic champion, but went on to beat Gerrie Coetzee for the WBA portion of the heavyweight pro title. Howard Davis Jnr also won a gold medal and was judged the best boxer in Montreal, guaranteeing him at least $1 million in pro earnings even though his jab-and-run strategy wasn't quite good enough for the pro ranks.

Jackson was one of the few Americans who didn't win a gold medal that year. In the pro ranks, he made it to the top five welterweights in the world only to find that his aggressive southpaw style wasn't good enough to beat the likes of Sugar Ray Leonard, Thomas Hearns or Donald Curry.

There was something distant in Jackson's eyes. A humble kind of sadness that told you in a look that he'd realised he wasn't quite good enough. He and Coffee and Johnny Bumphus had been the most successful trio from the one gym in American amateur fighting history. Together they'd won a total of more than 700 fights and had lost just 45. Bumphus won a world title, but Jackson failed. He was sure his protege

Kid Coffee would be a success.

Jackson used to fight as a welterweight. But when he arrived in Sydney he looked nothing like the tall, slim southpaw who shaped up the wrong way in the red, white and blue of the United States uniform.

He'd had a lifetime of experience in boxing. His weight was now maybe 50 pounds over his fighting best, but the excess was in hard muscle like the thick biceps that threatened to burst through his dark skin when he scratched the back of his head.

He was wearing his long, menacing goatee, his sensitive eyes hidden by black wraparound sunglasses and he had with him a wardrobe of t-shirts including a favourite that bore the message: "Got Ants in My Pants and Can't Dance". His nose meandered over his face like the Mississippi.

Most of the time the trainer let Coffee do the talking, slowly nodding his head to endorse the fighter's well-rehearsed answers.

"What planet is he from?" someone asked, loud enough to draw chuckles from other newsmen, but not so loud for the immovable Buddha to react. Jackson seldom spoke but when he did, in a high, soft voice, it was in reverent tones.

"This Fee-netch? Is that his name Fee-netch?" Jackson asked.

"Fee-neck," Coffee interrupted.

"This Mr Fee-netch is so easy to hit, well I bet when he sits down to eat his cornflakes for breakfast that spoon could leap right out of the bowl and wop him in the head. He's in for a boxin' lesson. Anything Fee-netch, can do, Jerome can do better. He's going to make Fee-netch ashamed of himself. Every fight you see, Fee-netch gets hit. He's so wide open. Against Jerome he'll pay."

Then Jackson retreated back into his brooding silence.

Stan Allen played the most serious role at the conference. Not for him, the excesses of hyperbole.

"We realise Jeff Fenech is a strong young champion, but we wonder whether he has the finesse to beat someone like Jerome. We're figuring he doesn't."

Allen had been to the title mountain before. Six months earlier he'd guided Diamond Jim McDonald to a world light-heavyweight title fight with soon-to-be-heavyweight champion Michael Spinks. Slim Jim went in eight.

Betty Sue Allen, a striking blonde whose primary function

was to attract publicity, cook meals for the troupe and call out "Tahm" every three minutes in the gym, said she loved "the excitement" of the sport. She didn't particularly care to see anyone bleed, she just hoped Jerome could beat Jeff without hurting him too much.

And then there was Kelvin Seabrooks. A 22-year-old who'd lost nearly as many fights as he'd won in a professional career that had seen him reduced to the status of opponent for every aspiring bantamweight in the States. They called him the Stinger because of his power-laden left hook. An inch or two shorter than the five-seven Coffee, Seabrooks had taken fights wherever he could get them, regardless of his chances.

He'd lost a points decision to Coffee in Nashville four years earlier and he'd told the press that nobody beats Jerome in Nashville. Now Seabrooks was Coffee's hired help. Ironically, two years later, with Coffee in temporary retirement, Seabrooks won the IBF bantamweight title after the scales told Fenech to move on and up.

"I've been sparring big guys," Coffee said, "I've been working with light-welterweights in preparation for this fight. Fee-neck is such a hitter, such a strong, aggressive fighter that it does my mind good to bust up those big guys in the gym. Kelvin is here to give me the razor's edge, to help me be in the best shape of my whole life. He's a real busy fighter — like Fee-neck but much more advanced."

Two months earlier Seabrooks had travelled with another former American amateur star, his friend, Bernard Taylor, to Belfast for a fight with Gaelic hero Barry McGuigan. Taylor was unbeaten in 34 fights, the master of hit-and-run fighting in the featherweight division. But after eight rounds he'd been unable to take any more body punches from the little Irishman.

As December 2 drew closer John Lewis would make comparisons between the styles of Taylor and Coffee. He'd predicted all along that the American, like Taylor, wouldn't be able to get into the trenches and fight toe-to-toe for a sustained period. On December 1 the video tape of Barry McGuigan-Bernard Taylor arrived at Fenech's cluttered Marrickville unit and the battle plan was approved. The sight of the tall, thin, quick man from North Carolina slowly but surely being sapped of all his strength and composure by thumping left hooks to the body, brought a devilish grin to Lewis' face and made Fenech that little bit closer to a sadistic peace-of-mind.

Coffee and his team spent their two weeks in Sydney camped in the top half of a luxury duplex overlooking the Pacific breakers at Coogee. They cooked their own meals or ate lobsters at a variety of seafood restaurants by the beaches, and spent much of their time endearing themselves to locals and displaying old fashioned hospitality and charm. Sure Coffee was a cocky loudmouth. But he honestly believed in his own destiny. He spoke mocking words to convince not only the Australian public but himself. He desperately wanted to beat Jeff Fenech. He never forgot watching Cassius Clay with his grandpa and how he'd always wanted to be the champ. Now he was getting his chance 25,000 kilometres from home and before an audience that would love to see his big mouth closed for good.

He was ever cheerful and optimistic. He displayed his tremendous hand speed and confidence in several training sessions at Ern McQuillan's gym. Sometimes keen students of the fight game would come away from his workouts saying that Fenech would have more to fear in Kelvin Seabrooks than in his talkative employer, that Coffee stretched too much when he threw his jab, that his right elbow kept coming away from his ribs, exposing a huge target for Fenech's left rip to the body. They said Coffee was fast but weak. Talented but frail. Others like McQuillan insisted Coffee would be too polished for a youngster like Fenech, that he was another Freddie Dawson. That he could box and punch. A fighter of genuine quality.

Coffee posed for photographs in front of a giant Tennessee flag he brought to Sydney for inspiration. He pinned a schedule of events to his living room wall: "Monday — Win Title, Tuesday — Party Time, Wednesday — Take Belt to USA".

Deep down Coffee knew his limitations. But he also knew the power of mind over muscle.

In the cellar of McQuillan's gym where Coffee would change his USA team t-shirt and shorts for a velvet USA boxing tracksuit, he'd tell listeners just how hard he'd dreamed to make his wishes come true.

"The thought of beating him gives me a high that I just can't explain. Many people dream of becoming a world champion at something, anything. Very few ever get the opportunity to grasp such an honour. If money was my motivation for fighting I'd have retired long ago. Pride in myself and my ability as a boxer has driven me for the last 15 years. That and the desire to be the best in the world at what I do.

"This is my one chance. Point blank. This is it."

Coffee also cruised Sydney Harbour and went to the local greyhound races, one of his favourite relaxations. There were times his mind needed a rest from the constant demands of self-motivation.

"Fee-neck," he would mutter, sometimes screech, in training. His theme song, "I've Got a New Attitude", Patti LaBelle's hit from the box office smash Beverly Hills Cop, would blast from his portable juke box and would provide the rhythm to accompany his sparring and bag punching sessions. He and Clint Jackson practised their routine daily, like brushing their teeth. Jackson would imitate the round-house rib assault Fenech had launched against Shingaki, and Coffee would catch the wide blows on his elbows and fore-arms, counter-punching with hard jabs and crosses to the punching pad Jackson held in front of his chin or in the area where Fenech's stomach was imagined to be. They'd gone through a similar routine for years, working out strategies to counter the styles of the 26 opponents Coffee had been paid to beat.

"Clint trained me so hard I thought he had some sort of vendetta against me," Coffee said, "I quit on him a few times along the way."

"Yeah," Jackson would interrupt, "I told him he could train like I said or he could hit the door. He hit the door. But he always bounced back."

Now Coffee just wanted to hit Fenech good and hard. A few days after arriving in Sydney, the challenger and champ passed each other running by the dawn's early light in the hundreds of acres in Centennial Park, the inner-city haven for joggers escaping concrete and smog.

"You'll have to run faster than that," Fenech shouted.

"My man, you will have to run faster to catch me," Coffee retorted.

It was light-hearted banter before the fight preparations would reach their most spiteful period.

Four days before the bout Fenech and Coffee sparred different opponents in the auditorium of the Newtown Police Youth Club where Shingaki had twice been an unwelcome visitor.

By then Coffee's best friend, a big black named Waldorf

"Mookie" Coleman had arrived in Sydney intent on playing his own mind games with the champion. Coffee was already at the gym with his trusty ghetto-blaster, blaring out his theme song when Mookie decided to draw first blood in the psychological warfare.

With hundreds of Fenech fans watching in the club he taped a photograph of Coffee with the words "Dear Jeff, thanks for the title" and "Coffee knocks out Fenech" scrawled across the smiling face. One of Fenech's sparring partners Brian Wilmott, grabbed the picture and tore it into shreds with all the venom of a mongoose throttling a cobra.

"____ dirty nigger ____," Fenech roared at Coleman, as cornermen restrained the Marrickville Mauler from staging a title fight then and there. Muhammad Ali used fake threats and mock fury to promote his multi-million dollar fights. But there was no mistaking Fenech's rage for any gimmick.

John Lewis was livid at his fighter's lapse in control.

"Cassius Clay did this crap all the time," he roared. "Ever since Coffee got here he's been mouthing off. He wants you rattled. He wants you as mad as hell and making mistakes. You do your talking after the fight."

Stan Allen was a distant observer. He liked the uncontrolled outburst from the champion because it hinted that Coffee could well fluster the youngster whose title they'd come to collect. Allen watched Fenech closely during the champion's workouts with Shane Knox and dismissed him as not being much better than when he fought Shingaki. Then he walked over to tell Coffee that he didn't have much to fear.

John Lewis pointed to his fighter's greater punching power and improved boxing skills as the deciding factors. He described Coffee as a perfect amateur, who like Bernard Taylor against McGuigan, would be found wanting in the rough stuff. A man who would be fast, but not fast enough to escape over 15 rounds of constant attack. The worst crashes are always in the fast lane.

On the eve of the bout, Coffee was philosophical.

"The good Lord above has looked down on me and given me the nod. He's said 'OK champ, it's your time now'. I don't hate this boy Fee-neck. But he has what I want. I expect him to come out winging, throwing his bombs early and then get frustrated in the middle of the fight. He'll start to make mistakes. Then I'll bust him up. I'm a boxer pure and simple, but I can rumble real good when I have to." ■

16
Coffee Breaks

"I am really willing to die in that ring. I'm obsessed with winning. I'm the champion of the world. My will is invincible. No man can defeat me"

Iron Mike Tyson, heavyweight champ 1987.

Now a lonely enemy in the crowded Sydney Entertainment Centre, Coffee needed to rumble real good. It was the start of round 12 and Fenech's relentless aggression had him way out in front on the judges' scorecards. For the first nine rounds, save for the opening two minutes of the first, Coffee had been unable to show what he'd promised.

In his dressing room before the fight he'd told Stan Allen to wrap his hands tight because he wanted Fee-neck to know he'd been hit hard.

In the champion's room, Fenech told Clint Jackson, supervising as Lewis bandaged Fenech's hands, that he'd now see how easy it was to make that cornflakes spoon miss.

Fenech had wanted to rumble straight away. In fact he even jumped the start, marching straight towards Coffee even before the bell for round one. But he met more than he bargained for.

Coffee's long hard, straight left snaked out again and again, to the head, to the body, and back to the head again. His long punches may not have been as damaging as Fenech's, but they were accurate and worrying stings. Midway through the round Coffee tried his creamer. A roundhouse abbreviated loop that missed by a country mile. Then Coffee tried out his left hook and it landed like a hand grenade exploding inside Fenech's head. This was going to be harder than the champion thought. Just like the street fighting days he grabbed Coffee, picked him up, and threw him into the ropes. If Rudy Battle, the referee, hadn't been there Fenech would have dumped the deputy sheriff out of the ring.

"Coffee is a good technician," Barry Michael informs the TV audience estimated to be more than a million people in Australia and on delay, 39 million in the United States. "But Jeff should just keep on the pressure."

The chants of "Fenech! Fenech!" are starting to echo among the noise of 12,074 voices crying in the darkness. Together they've made the Fenech-Coffee fight the biggest single money-spinner at the Entertainment Centre and there is no doubt where their loyalties lie.

Grace Jones, the singer with the menacing public persona, is at ringside with her towering lover Dolph Lundgren, Stallone's fearsome Russian rival, Ivan Drago, in Rocky IV.

In the second round Coffee lands with his creamer, but Fenech has swallowed more than that on the streets. The champion grabs Coffee in a head-lock and throws a punch behind his own back at Coffee's trapped face. Referee Battle, an American at the centre of controversy, is already starting to push Fenech away from Coffee in the clinches. The champion later complains that Battle sapped some of his strength by always pushing him when it was Coffee who was constantly holding on.

"Coffee is surprised at Fenech's strength," Michael remarks, "Jeff will make him fight as the bout goes further."

Before the start of the third Coffee is in noticeable distress, struggling with his over-sized black mouthguard that makes his lips protrude like an African Mick Jagger. While he is gagging on the offending plastic, Fenech rushes across the ring with a right cocked, ready to kill, only to see the challenger jump to one side. Fenech chases and catches, picking Coffee up again and throwing him into the ropes for a second time.

"No wrestlin', no wrestlin', no wrestlin'. Clean contest," says Battle, who has clearly taken over from Nashville's mouth of the south.

At the end of the third Coffee is showing the first signs of pain and his dancing retreat moves into full gear. Fenech won't be stopped from doing what he does best — hurting other people.

At the end of the sixth, frustrated by Coffee's clinching and snarling at the referee for continually pushing him away, Fenech walks head-first into Coffee's face, a gesture that prompts continued fighting after the bell and a caution for both fighters.

"By separating them all the time the referee is nullifying Jeff's in-fighting," Michael explains.

In Fenech's corner Lewis is imploring his boxer not to throw the title away.

"Don't let these blokes rattle you," he says of both Coffee and Battle, "Stay calm. Beat this bloke on ability. No more head butts."

For the next four rounds, Fenech blossoms and Coffee wilts. The challenger spends most of the 12 minutes going backwards, swatting at the on-rushing champion and constantly missing as Fenech sets out to prove he can box as well as brawl.

Coffee isn't about to give in without giving Fenech the fight of his life.

In the 10th round the American hammers over his best punch of the fight. A right hand that has all his 118 pounds of sinew and bone behind it. It isn't the Coffee Creamer but something stronger and straighter.

Fenech is hurt.

"That's the first time we've seen Jeff a little shaken," Michael says, "Coffee came here to take the title. He's breathing well. He's looking very confident, but he really must come home strong."

Now it is the start of round 12 and Jerome's black and silver sequinned trunks are dripping with the sweat of hard labour. Four rounds to go. Four rounds to land that one good right hand he knew would win him the title he had dreamed of with his grandpa.

Fenech starts the 12th in the role of the matador. He has been the bull for most of the fight, but after being struck by the sharp horns, he has no desire to tempt his luck a second time. It is his turn to retreat and cover up and let Coffee strive for the kill. Fenech draws Coffee in. Now Jerome is wide open, now he is winging them, hoping to end it. Now he is the aggressive comer.

It's the opening Fenech wants. Now he will rumble real good. A left hook has Coffee hanging on again and Battle sprinting in to separate them as a dissatisfied mob starts to boo. Fenech traps Coffee in a corner and at last Jerome knows he is beaten. The promised Tennessee rumble has crumbled. His place with Cassius Clay has been stolen by the rookie who got to Shingaki first.

"Coffee is hurt, Coffee is hurt," Michael is shouting. And he is. Like a kid's golliwog he is limp and lifeless, a rag doll being tossed around the ring, hurled this way and that. The bull has changed his mask again.

"How strong is this man Fenech?" Michael continues, "Absolutely fantastic, Jeff Fenech is all over Coffee like the tax collector. He's a freak. His strength is incredible. Definitely beyond human."

In the 13th Coffee complains about low blows and almost falls over in his struggle to keep Fenech at a distance.

Coffee's arms may only have the strength of paper in the last round but all of his 15 years in boxing have gone in to another right hand. With the clock beating him to the finish, he is still looking for that knockout. It won't come. For nearly three minutes Fenech slips Coffee's desperation blows, shooting back his own accurate jab and occasional body shots. Ten seconds from the end, Coffee lands a brute of a left hook that sends Fenech's arms flailing.

But too late. Much too late.

The bell. A weary embrace. John Lewis marches around the ring arms in the air. He says that for the last hour he's been in orbit, oblivious to everything except for the tightly-muscled fighter in the green and gold shorts.

"May your reign be long," Coffee whispers in to the champion's ear, 12 hours before demanding a rematch.

"I thought you'd get tired, I thought you'd punch yourself out after 10. But I was wrong. You surprised me. You're a hell of a fighter."

Clint Jackson is dabbing a coagulent on Coffee's torn skin around the right eye. Stan Allen is shaking hands with Fenech's handlers. All three judges are awarding Fenech a clear-cut victory.

Paul Fenech, who felt Coffee's last two desperation punches every bit as much as his champion son, was smiling. Jeff Fenech is telling the world he proved that he can box; that he proved he is a worthy titleholder. He and Lewis embrace as they had done after every fight.

"In four years Johnny has taught me more than anyone else could have shown me in 20," Fenech says. "I really love the bloke. I'd be nothing without him." ■

17
A Friend In Need

"The day you forget the people who helped you is the day they forget you"
                                                            <u>Jeff Fenech, 1988</u>

Humour in times of adversity has always been a trademark of the romantic hero and it's been evident in the mystique and charisma surrounding Australia's most popular and successful boxer.

Forty-eight hours before he would cross gloves with the fighter who would once and for all prove Fenech had star quality, the world champ was flat on his back in his hotel suite bed, wearing a South Sydney football guernsey, a pair of bathing trunks, long white socks and with a telephone cradled to his ear.

"Hello. Would Con Spyropoulos be there please?" he asks in an accent somewhere between Eton and Sydney's North Shore. Of course Con Spyropoulos is there. He's been asleep in the next room not more than 10 feet away on the other side of a pink pastel wall.

"Oh is that you, Con?" Fenech continues, warming to his impersonation, "This is Bruce Robertson from Channel 7. We're compiling a special report on this hot young boxing talent Jeff Fenech and we'd like to ask you some questions about this wonderful fellow.

"First, Con, what is Jeff Fenech like? . . . A very nice boy? Yes we thought so too. Is he a very good fighter? . . . The best? I see, And who is he fighting on Friday night? . . . Daniel Zaragoza. Ah hah. Tell me Con what will Jeff Fenech do to this Zaragoza? . . . Knock him right out, eh? What's that? . . . And break his jaw? Right, yes, I understand.

"Okay Con, now it's very important that I talk to Jeff Fenech because I've got a few questions to ask him too. Is Jeff there, Con? . . . He is? . . . Oh I see, he's asleep. Well I'm sure

"

he won't mind if you wake him up . . . No, no, Con, I don't think Jeff Fenech has a bad temper, he's a very nice boy. Yes. It is very, very important that I speak to Jeff Fenech tonight . . . Yes, I know he's getting ready for a big fight but unless we talk to him tonight we won't be able to put our program on the TV.

"Oh then you will wake him up? . . . Very good, Con. Thank you very much . . . Yes, yes I'll hold the line."

As soon as Fenech utters the word "line" he hangs up his phone, leaps under the covers, tells a friend sharing the joke to make like he's asleep in an armchair, and starts loud and exaggerated snoring. So loud in fact that it muffles the whispers coming from the open doorway into Fenech's room.

"Hey, Jeff," a voice hushes around the corner as the head and body hides from view. A little louder: "Hey, Jeff." Louder still but not loud enough to stop the snoring: "Hey, Jeff."

Ever so tentatively Con snakes around the architrave; "Hey, Jeff, phone, mate." Fenech keeps snoring from beneath his lair of blankets and pillows with one dark eye open just a sliver to survey his handiwork.

Con Spyropoulos grows in courage and inches forward, closer to where his boxing champ mate lies concealed.

A yell: "Hey, Jeff. The bloody phone, mate."

Fenech stirs from his feigned slumber with an invented and passable attempt at drowsiness. He puts on a look like he's just drunk a whole bottle of cod liver oil, stares blankly for a few seconds at a digital clock which says its near enough to midnight, shifts his incredulous gaze to his chubby pal dressed in blue shorty pyjamas and drops his jaw a full six inches.

And then in a voice deliberately hoarse: "What are you jibberin' about, Con? Can't you tell the bloody time, ya flip." Con can't but Fenech has convinced him that half past three is just the same as a quarter to eight. Con lives in a world with no time and no pressures. Sometimes Fenech says he is better off without faculties than people who live in high anxiety. Con always seems to have a good time.

He is undeterred. "The phone, Jeff," he whines. "A bloke wants an interview."

"An interview? What, at this time?" Fenech shouts back in exasperation. "It's 12 o'clock at night. I've got a big fight lined up. Do you want Zaragoza to bash me or what?"

"Na, Jeff," Con continues with the voice of a kid explaining why he hasn't done his homework, "Honest, Jeff, he's on the phone. He's from that place, Jeff — what do ya call it?"

"What place?"

"You know Channel 7." Con's eyes roll toward the roof.

"It's 12 o'clock at night, Con," Fenech growls, "What kind of bastard would ring someone up at 12 o'clock in the night?"

Con gets more frantic with Fenech's continued interrogation, but in the end the champ relents.

"All right, Con, I'm going into your room, but this better not be another practical joke or I'll rip you up ya fat guts."

Fenech marches into Con's bedroom with his five feet four, 15 stone retarded best mate ambling behind. He snatches up the phone dangling by a dishevelled bed.

"Hello," Pause. "Hello." Another pause. "Is there anyone there?" He holds the phone roughly to Con's ear so he too can listen to the lifeless dial tone. Then with Con's un-comprehending face staring at him, Fenech slams the phone down wheels around to his startled friend and starts shaping up. He ducks and weaves and bobs the same way he did when he came out smokin' against Percy Israel in his second pro-fessional fight. Only this time he's throwing feathers instead of bombs.

"I warned you about this shit when you did it to me last night," Fenech snarls, "Now I'm gonna make sure you don't do it again."

Con screams something incoherent and stumbles over his own feet, collapsing on his bed like some giant water bomb. Fenech takes four steps backward and with a running start leaps high into the air and comes down in a bellyflop with a blood-curdling scream of "It's the Hulkster." Con is letting fly with more four letter words than at a bullock drivers' bucks night.

In between repeated wrestling and sparring sessions Fenech has taught Con, brain-damaged since birth, to repeat hundreds of phrases, some of them not so aesthetic to the ear, and says he has helped Con come out of his shell and enjoy life more. He says he's been good for Con the same way Con's been good for him.

For 10 minutes or so the pair wrestle on the bed and on the floor of the bedroom with Con roaring like a wounded buffalo. Fenech gets the upper hand, alternating his attack with a whole variety of tricks and holds including the sleeper lock, the half nelson and the dreaded Boston crab. He tells Con he'd give him a brain buster only there's not much there to bust.

"What's up there?" he asks, tapping Con's bald spot.

"Sawdust?" Con replies, "Light's on, but nobody's home to keep the burglars away."

After feigning bites and eye gouges on an opponent whose best defence is kicking and punching the same way a girl throws a softball, the impromptu wrestling match ends in a no contest. The phone is ringing again.

The hotel manager. And this time it's no joke.

"Yes, sir, I'm sorry about the noise," Fenech explains in the little kid voice that gets used often in similar situations. "What happened was that Con was having a shower and he slipped on the soap and banged his head. I ran in from my room when I heard him fall. Poor bastard was screamin' 'is head off. I tried to calm 'im down but he just wouldn't shut up. It took me ages to get him quiet. What's that? Oh no, no. It won't happen again. I'll keep an eye on him. Thank you very much. Thank you. Good night."

Within five minutes Con has told Fenech he loves him and within 10 he is tucked in to bed, asleep and snoring louder than Fenech could with a microphone.

"I don't know what I'd do without Costa (Fenech's nickname for Con)," the champion says after peace and order have been restored to the hotel suite and the hours tick away toward his fight with the best bantamweight in Mexico.

"Without him to have a laugh with I'd probably go insane."

When he was a boy of 10 or so Con, bigger than two 10-year-olds put together and so very different from the other kids in Marrickville, used to chase Fenech and his footballing pal Bronko Djura, now a first grade rugby league player in Sydney, everyday after school. Fenech was terrified of the big kid with the stumbling gait.

It was some weeks before Con and Bronko de Genius — Con's way of pronouncing Djura — realised the big kid with the stupid grin and the difficulties with his speech, was only trying to make friends. From that day on a bizarre and fascinating friendship developed between hoodlum and handicapped. Fenech would take Con wherever he went — to the beach, to mates' houses, to the local pool, on dates and finally to the Newtown Police Youth Club. Every Christmas they'd chase a particularly fat, red-faced man who was the local Santa Claus down busy Illawarra Road with Fenech and Con hand in hand shouting "Hey Santa how 'bout some presents, ya bloody Irish wog".

"I started taking Con to the gym with me because I thought it would be good for him to mix with a lot of people at once and maybe it could help him with his speech problems," Fenech said. "Con was very shy around other people at first, but it didn't take long before he became just another one of the boys. Everyone treated him the same as everyone else and his speech started to improve. His confidence around people grew all the time.

"In the end Con started to boss us all around. I reckon I've also helped Con develop greater self-confidence by getting him to climb into the ring with me after every fight. That's not a publicity thing or anything like that because Con is my mate and I could never take advantage of him. I used to drag him into the ring to wave at the crowd when I was fighting in the clubs and there was hardly anyone there to watch. He's so heavy that it used to take three of us to drag him into the ring before he learnt how to climb through the ropes by himself. Now I couldn't stop Con getting into the ring with me even if I wanted to. He'd knock me right out if I tried. Con's even turned into a bit of a lair. He goes to all the fights telling everyone he's a celebrity. He probably signs more autographs than I do."

Con's star status is a fitting reward for the convincing, yet unwitting, public relations job he performed in making a nation believe that boxing, long comatose in Australia, was not so brutal and archaic. There was, after all, a human side.

And even though the pair of them acted like big, overgrown kids in the lead-up to Fenech's toughest test to that time against Zaragoza, Con also helped the world boxing champion develop greater emotional maturity. Despite the imminent showdown with the fighter who would take everything Fenech had to offer and keep coming back for more, Fenech was more relaxed before their April, 1986 fight than he had been for a dozen easier contests.

More the 5000km from home in the West Australian capital of Perth, preparing to fight before an untested audience and against an unshakeable tough, Fenech was looking forward to the Zaragoza fight like a five-year-old waiting for Christmas. There were several reasons why.

The bout was being fought at a weight limit of 123 pounds instead of the bantamweight maximum of 118 pounds and so,

for one of the few times in his career, Fenech could have a few
mouthfuls of food in the days before the bout. His relationship with Lewis was flourishing again after the traumas of
1985 had been dissolved. There was the presence of Con
Spyropoulos, ever available to a joust or jest like a puppy with
a stick. Always prepared, with Fenech's prodding, to whack
someone on the back of the head and run.

As well as being a sparring partner of sorts and a faithful
sidekick, Con also helps fulfil Fenech's constant, almost critical, need for company. The champion cannot bear to be by
himself. Maybe it's a legacy from the days when his dad was
so often in hospital and his mum always away trying to make
ends meet. Whether he be with Con or Lewis, Mario Fenech
or Bronko de Genius or any number of kids he employs to
carry his bags and run his errands, loneliness is something
Fenech never wants to know.

Just as his boxing career was beginning to flourish, Fenech
would boast that he'd never need to work in his life because
there were enough friends who would always provide for him.
Friends are the reason he didn't go completely off the rails
years ago.

And there's always the telephone to fall back on. In Perth
in the hours before Zaragoza, it was rarely off the hook, a
giant lifeline to friends and lovers back home. Sometimes in
the middle of the night he'd get the urge to phone a trainer he
didn't like somewhere in the world, posing as an overseas promoter who'd eventually turn the conversation with his dazed,
just woken victims to finding their opinions on "the greatest
bantamweight in the world." Those who claimed Fenech
wasn't worth a stamp or was an "over-rated smart-arse" who
only fought bums and has-beens, would be marked down in
his memory bank for another call in the early hours next
morning.

Being away from Sydney for a couple of weeks in Perth,
where the America's Cup was still the biggest talking point,
also gave Fenech time to relax and to rehearse new routines
with Con. Routines of rote designed to give him a mental edge
over his rivals. Over and over again he'd teach Con to call his
intended victims names like Daniel Sarsparilla or he'd get
Con to sprout "Jerome Coffee is a dog" or to prance around
with fingers stretching his eyes into an Oriental caricature
before the Shingaki and Payakarun slaughters.

Humour with a knife edge has long been Fenech's way of

convincing himself he has nothing to fear in a sport where someone's always going to get hurt. The mind games he plays before a fight are almost as intricate as the moves and counter-moves he takes into the ring.

At a civic reception with coats, ties, pearls and champagne for all but the two most important people, Fenech was introduced to the battle-hardened Zaragoza for the first time a few days before their 10-round fight at the cavernous Perth Entertainment Centre.

Such a meeting would have been like suggesting the champion dress up in drag in the days when the Marrickville Mauler could not go into a fight without malice toward the other little bloke in the opposite corner. But the new look Jeff Fenech had a whole new attitude by the time he arrived in Perth.

When Zaragoza came down from Mexico City to prove he still had the goods, Fenech was well aware his own ability needed no condiments. Except maybe a cheap shot or two.

Peeved that he had to be dressed in a collar and tie when he'd much rather have been sleeping back at his hotel, Fenech looked across at Zaragoza's weathered face, with the big flattened nose and let him have it with both barrels.

"Hey, look at you," Fenech said, the grin betraying his plans for a rival who never learned English when he was learning to live on the streets of Mexico City. "What a melon. Anyone told ya you've got a head like a busted arse?" Zaragoza didn't know whether Fenech was wishing him good luck or commenting on the weather, but in Fenech's constantly scheming mind he'd already chalked up the first round.

But while Fenech tried to turn on the slapstick, the wiry Mexican with the big target on his shoulders, was in no laughing mood.

He came to Australia to end Fenech's winning streak and gain another world title shot at the expense of the comparatively inexperienced Australian. Zaragoza was clearly the toughest, bravest fighter Fenech had ever met and like Farrell and Shingaki he was probably possessed of more raw courage than was good for his health. He also had a permanent sneer etched onto his "melon" and eyes like Sonny Liston's that could stare right down into the soul. He gave the impression that years ago, in the sprawling, festering sore of a Mexico City slum, someone had swiped his marbles and he'd been filthy on the world ever since.

Above: Paul and Mary Fenech gave their boy a fighting start in life.

Right: A Fenech family group including uncles and aunts before Jeff was born. Paul and Mary (at the back of this family group) had five children before Jeff. They were (clockwise from bottom right) Rita, Godfrey, Eric, Henry and Veronica.

John and Lorrie McEnearney became Fenech's advisers and patrons.

Samart Payakarun slipped this big right hand but he caught enough to end up in hospital

Right: Three world titles, a sore hand and a happy face after stopping Victor Callejas for the WBC featherweight title - Photo: Gary Chapman, The Daily Telegraph. Below: Fenech trained for the fight at Aanuka Beach, Coffs Harbor, with Grantlee Kieza (left), Lewis and great friend Mitchell Barnes. Photo: Wayne Jones, Daily Mirror.

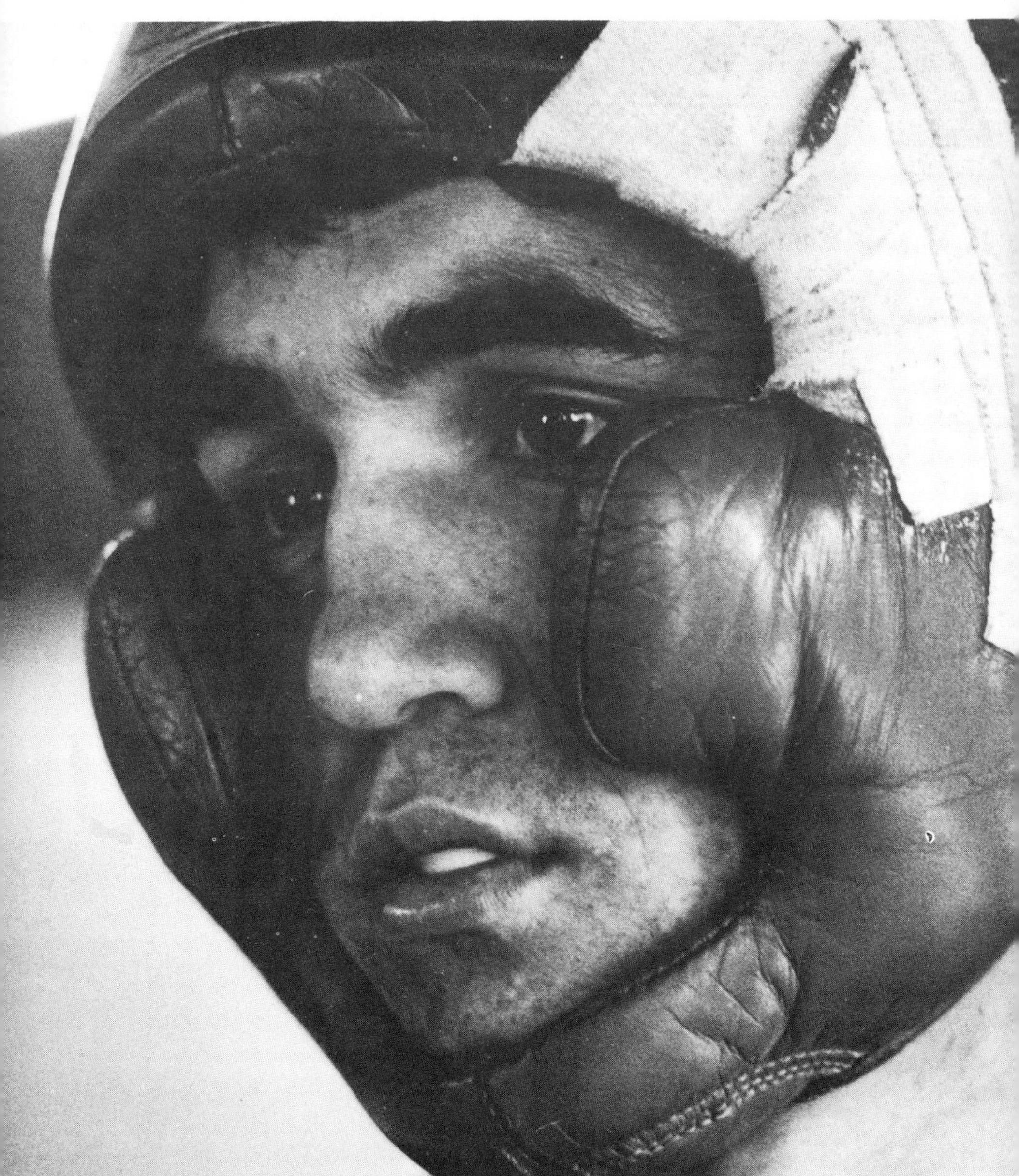

Underneath, the exterior of a
great boxer is a complex
personality — a dozen different
people in one. And all of them
can fight.

Like Farrell, Shingaki and Rolly Navarro, Zaragoza was also left-handed. He could hurt an opponent with everything he threw and knock them out with most. He came from a long line of Mexican toughs. His father was said to have fought 400 times as a professional and his brother Augustin had won a bronze medal at Zaragoza's home town Olympics in 1968. He had started the long and dangerous road of a boxing career as an amateur at the age of 20 when most of his peers had been fighting for years. He had boxed at the 1980 Moscow Olympics and despite two points losses to American Harold Petty, he had captured the WBC bantamweight crown in 1985 when another American, Freddie Jackson, was disqualified in their bout for the vacant championship on the Caribbean Island resort of Aruba.

Zaragoza had suffered his third loss in 31 fights when he was knocked down three times in the fourth and fifth rounds and outpointed against Colombian Migual Lora in losing the title in Miami. He ended up half way round the world in Perth hoping to earn a shot at the heavier world super-bantamweight crown by beating Fenech.

Lewis never really wanted his fighter to take on Zaragoza. Sure enough, the win over Coffee before a packed house four months earlier, proved Fenech could outfight a tricky, world-class stylist with a pesky left jab. But compared to Zaragoza, Coffee was feather-fisted. The Mexican slugger was one of the big boys from the country where inept fighters ended up back with the millions in squalor.

At first Lewis believed Zaragoza would be far too great a risk for Fenech. Too big, too strong and much too experienced and brutal for a kid with only a dozen pro starts on his slate. But after watching Zaragoza bounce off the floor against Lora on video tape he decided Fenech could beat the Mexican with a single punch — his left jab.

"Zaragoza is certainly tough enough," Lewis said, explaining his decision to throw Fenech into the deep end after deciding he could survive in shark-infested waters.

"Anyone who gets off the floor three times and is able to come back strong in the late rounds has to have a big heart. But by the same token, anyone who is on the floor three times in the space of two rounds has to be easy to hit. If they're standing in front of him asking for it, Jeff will catch them every time."

Fenech's improved level of maturity manifested itself in his preparation in his dressing room before the fight.

He no longer needed to brood. The catatonic state, the self-induced trance and malevolent stare were no longer needed. Instead he cracked jokes with a young and nervous television sportscaster making his first live report and he signed autographs and patted kids' heads. He no longer needed to convince himself that he could fight.

Minutes before he would stake his credibility on the line and march out before the expectant crowd and the multitude watching at home wondering if he could really tough it out with a man who'd been a world champion a few months earlier, Fenech was treating the whole episode like just another day in the gym.

But once the fighting started, it was time to get serious and show the other side of his erratic nature which he'd been supressing for weeks.

It was unlucky for Fenech that his 13th fight would be held in a wrestling ring, the same ring in which, a night earlier, Mr Fuji, an insidious but dapper Oriental villain, had opened someone's skull with a walking stick. The ring's extra padding and loosened ropes prevented Fenech from inflicting similar injuries on Zaragoza. Even though he did his best.

The Mexican strongman lived up to his fearsome reputation as he set about trying to knock Fenech out with every punch he threw. If he'd been able to land with a flurry, instead of only the sporadic slap shot Fenech occasionally allowed through his defence, he probably would have earned that second world title shot straight away.

But all along Lewis had said Zaragoza would be too slow with both hands and feet to catch his ever-improving champion. Most of Zaragoza's punches were sent by morse code. Even the audience knew when they were coming by the time he'd planted his feet, gritted his teeth and loaded up his fists like double nought cartridges in a shotgun. Only in the sixth did he land with any sequence of hurtful blows, but by that time, Fenech had the adrenalin pumping so fast there was no turning back.

Although Zaragoza was ringwise enough from his 31 previous fights to slip many of Fenech's cannon blasts in close, Fenech was continually able to bully the Mexican around the ring the same way he'd outmuscled rivals since his rudimentary boxing beginnings. To his shock and chagrin, Zaragoza found himself out-toughed and out-boxed by a dogged kid he thought was just a pup.

But he still wasn't prepared to give in. Unable to land with many effective legal punches, he tried everything in the black book — low blows, an elbow to the chin when he'd miss with the hook, cutting laces cuffed across Fenech's face. And all he got back for his efforts was a Fenech thumb in the eye and the most numbing, most blatant and most vicious head-butt Fenech has ever landed. If Zaragoza hadn't initiated the rough stuff, Fenech would probably have been disqualified.

For much of the fight Fenech was able to land at will. Zaragoza should have gone down any number of times and he certainly had good reason to call an end to the one-way traffic of punches coming his way. He would have called it quits, but for that extraordinary part of his psyche that kept telling his legs to remain firm.

Fenech won by a landslide decision. It was a monstrous mauling of a fighter who came to Perth with a giant-sized reputation and went home feeling like a cracked shell.

After almost every fight before Zaragoza, the champion had greeted victory with an arrogant, triumphal march around the roped perimeters of the ring he controlled. Strutting his stuff with arms held high and his emotions gushing out in a long stream of unabashed narcissism like a dog which has been chained for days and is finally free.

But after he'd proved himself on the international scene at last, with a complete and comprehensive win over Zaragoza, Fenech greeted the judges' decision with a mere shrug of his shoulders, a simple acknowledgment of the applause and a great debt of gratitude to his friends.

This was a victory to really savour. If only his damn hand didn't hurt so much.■

18

Olympic Revenge

> *"When he got in trouble in the ring, Ali*
> *imagined a door swung open and inside he*
> *could see neon, orange and green lights*
> *blinking and bats blowing trumpets and*
> *alligators playing trombones and snakes*
> *screaming"*
>
> George Plimpton, US writer.

For the first time in his five-year boxing career, the world champion looked like he had been in a fight. For the first time in a career which had taken him around the world and into a nation's heart, he had been asked to pay a terrible price. He looked like a battered pug should look.

Lying on the floor of an unfurnished bedroom in the Erskineville home he had recently commissioned near the Police Boys' Club, Fenech was buried under a pile of blankets. the telephone once again grafted to his ear. Friends were with him, standing by his bedside like he were some great general wounded in battle. Joe Aquilina, who first met Fenech as his sponsor, but soon became like a brother, Mario Fenech and Peter Mitrevski. All there to help the soothing. A night earlier they had winced and twitched through every blow as Fenech had pounded out a 14-round upset over Steve McCrory. It was an upset because it was never supposed to be so hard.

"Of course I'm talkin' funny," Fenech said into the mouthpiece to a friend miles away, "I just got my head bashed in. Remember? I've still got brain damage." He actually had a cold, which compounded his many woes. The flippancy was a translucent screen over the awful truth. For the first time in a fight he came away looking like a loser.

Both of Fenech's eyes had swollen into slits like John Farrell's a year earlier when it was Fenech doling out all the aches and pains. This time it was the champion who had emerged from the fight with one side of his face red and distorted. The other side was purple. Fenech's jaw had swollen dramatically, as though sometime during the fight promoter Bill Mordey had predictably tagged "Olympic Revenge," he had contracted the mumps. Worst of all, his left hand had finally and completely betrayed him. Now his fist was black and swollen with a pain which had soured what should have been the sweetest and most satisfying victory in his time of fighting.

A night earlier, five minutes after he had shown McCrory and the boxing world what he and Ed Weichers had predicted since their Olympic preparation together, Fenech had been crying his swollen eyes out. Not because he was especially overjoyed at having, at last, exorcised the evil spirits that had plagued him since he walked away from the travesty against Redzepovski. And not just because the win over McCrory was the proudest moment he and John Lewis had shared since he'd left Shingaki reeling around the ring at the Hordern Pavilion. Fenech was crying because of pain. Sheer pain that cut through him like no opponent had ever done before.

For 14 rounds against McCrory, Fenech had gritted his teeth and pushed the agony of his hand damage into the darkest corner of his mind. He had bludgeoned the American around the ring until Paul Moore, the referee, had no alternative but to drag him away from an opponent whose resistance had wilted long before his hopes of at least seeing out the distance.

But when the fight was over and Fenech, the boxer capable of so much animal-like ferocity, no longer had to behave like a beast, all of his defensive mechanisms collapsed. Unashamed, he wept with pain. Blubbering like a five-year old who has scraped his knees on playground concrete.

From the time he won his first Australian amateur title in Melbourne three years before, Fenech's left hand had conspired against him with the right. The left was always the real troublemaker. Ever since that first championship in Melbourne.

His hands have been mis-shapen since birth and he became a world boxing champion incapable of making a true fist. When he closed his fingers together, the index finger of each hand would poke out from the others in a point. When he landed with a punch, and his left jab has always been his most frequent form of attack, most of the blow's force was taken on the pointed index finger leaving his knuckles bruised and swollen.

After Fenech had dispatched McCrory in a fight that had been one-sided, his left index finger swelled to the size and colour of a plump barbecued sausage. He spent the time usually allotted for jubilation in his dressingroom crying and moaning. At the post-fight party, in an ante-room at the Sydney Entertainment Centre, he spent the time propped against the bar like a drunk, too tired to move and barely able to speak. He farewelled friends and well-wishers with muffled mutterings through fat lips, his face already adopting the distorted contours it would bear for the next week or two.

Now lying on the floor of a bedroom awaiting a bed, Fenech was able to joke with a friend by telephone about the occupational hazards of his profession and what it was doing to his grey matter. The sport had given him so much during the past five years. Now it was asking for something back.

"He sure hurt me a few times," Fenech told his mates watching over him, "But his best shots were like mossie bites compared to the pain I felt everytime I whacked him back. It was like someone was shoving a knife right through my fist."

The most painful part of all was that McCrory was supposed to be an easy victim. Olympic Revenge was the ultimate exploitation of a good idea to its storybook end. Robbed in Los Angeles by powers beyond his control, by officials who hid behind their rules, Fenech was supposed to batter McCrory from post to post as quickly as possible and put the whole gold medal debate finally to rest. McCrory was given the battering, but not before he had proved himself to be far more dangerous than Fenech had expected.

The Fenech-McCrory bout was the fight all Australia — at least that section of the country with only passing interest in the career of its most famous boxer — had wanted to see.

As his professional record had mushroomed and his popularity skyrocketed, Fenech's greatest selling point to the public and his most tempting bait for media attention had been the despair of Los Angeles. Paul Fenech had long believed the controversy of the Olympics had been the spark which ignited his son's explosive professional career. Without Redzepovski, the road to Shingaki would have been longer and much more demanding.

The spectre of that little Slavic gypsy and the jury that

voted for him despite so much evidence to the contrary, was responsible for as many subsequent ticket sales to Fenech fights as brute strength and killer instinct put together.

Since he burst into tears at the press conference following his catastrophic quarter-final, Fenech had sworn to his gradually growing army of followers that he could have walked right through McCrory if those "senile old men" had not ruined everything. Olympic Revenge gave Fenech the chance to put his fists where McCrory's mouth was. Fenech's smouldering rage, which no amount of professional success or its subsequent wealth could dampen, and the skills of the man who ended up with the gold medal and the highest position on the victory dais, would be finally locked together in a 15-round fight for the better man to prove himself.

Everyone connected with Fenech knew who would win. They'd been certain of it ever since McCrory had coasted through the third round to a split points decision over Redzepovski in the Olympic final. He may have been a world amateur champion and an Olympic gold medallist, but as a professional, McCrory had done little to encourage hopes of beating Fenech. Despite his deserved reputation as a master of the amateur style, little Stevie was held in little regard by students of professional boxing.

In Los Angeles, McCrory's gold medal-winning performance had been overshadowed by the more spectacular performances of his team-mates like Mark Breland, Sweet Pea Whittaker, Meldrick Taylor and Tyrell Biggs and by the disqualification of Evander Holyfield, a controversy even greater than that of the Fenech-Redzepovski match. As a professional, McCrory had grown accustomed to fighting in the long shadow and on the undercards to his brother Milton, the exciting welterweight the press called the Ice Man, and who until his chilling knockout loss to Donald Curry in 1985, was the WBC world champion. The elder McCrory had made several million dollars from boxing because of the frequency with which he was able to stiffen challengers.

The Ring magazine, for 66 years the Bible of boxing, had lamented Steve McCrory's apparent lack of strength. "He has already had to endure a draw, a knockdown and a number of so-so outings," the magazine said some months before McCrory's arrival in Australia. "He laboured to outpoint Luigi Camputaro and was knocked down and clearly hurt by Karry Allen. The way it looks so far, Steve, while highly skilled, just doesn't have the strength to compete with bantamweights."

Together with a videotape of McCrory going the distance with the laughable Kenny Butts, the evidence was enough to convince John Lewis that Fenech would have sizeable amounts of revenge and reward.

At least that was the thinking until Fenech's left hand, still sore from 10 tough rounds when it was almost always in contact with Daniel Zaragoza's face and body, forced postponements of Olympic Revenge from May 23 to June 20 and then, finally, to July 18. The hand damage would severely limit Fenech's preparation for his third title defence and his lack of proper training would ultimately prove telling.

McCrory's boxing career started when he was nine years old. He and big brother Milton, and a neighbourhood chum named Jimmy Paul, had all headed off together to learn boxing in a local Detroit gym. Little Stevie had always been the most brilliant student. He may not have had the leverage or the power of his lanky brother, nor the crunching right cross Jimmy Paul would develop as a patient and deadly counterpuncher, but he could box just like the textbook intended. Jab, counterpunch, slip and slide. He could do it all. Milton spoke about his brother's talent like an art buff extolling the virtues of the Renaissance masters. His brother's skills, he said, were "God given" — there was a beauty, a preciousness to the subtle way he could make an opponent miss and come back with counters from all angles.

By the time Olympic Revenge neared, it became apparent that McCrory was not just fighting for the riches and fame a world title would bring. He had a greater motive. He was fighting to establish his own identity. Milton and Jimmy Paul, whose potent right took him to the IBF lightweight title, had both reached the top of their profession. Yet the younger McCrory, the most gifted of the trio, remained anonymous to all but the most committed fight fan or Olympic historian. As far as most Americans were concerned, he was just someone in the small print in the records section of Olympic history. Nothing much to get excited about.

Little Stevie had grown tired of living in his brother's Detroit mansion, preferring to move his wife and daughter into a place of their own. Long before he stepped into the ring to fight Fenech, McCrory had become fed up with only reading about the other gold medallists from Los Angeles. He drove the latest car and wore the latest styles, but he was frustrated and restless.

If McCrory could whip Fenech, whip him good, he would not only beat Breland and the other LA gold medallists to a world title, but he would, once and for all, step out of his brother's spotlight and into the one aimed directly at him.

Steve McCrory arrived in style to prepare for Olympic Revenge. His flyweight gold medal, the central issue in the debate over who was the better fighter, shone brightly from around his neck when he walked into his first Australian press conference at Sydney Airport. It was an obvious publicity stunt, but it had the desired effect of further hyping what many expected to be a mismatch.

Even though he had been a world leader in amateur boxing and had spent his adolescence surrounded by gloved luminaries at Detroit's world famous Kronk Gym, McCrory was overawed by the attention he created. His gold medal display and his first day in front of the microphones and cameras would be one of the rare occasions he'd actually have something to say about the biggest fight of his life.

McCrory described "Fentch" as a "brawler" and "not much of a thinker". He said he'd heard that "Fentch" was "always cryin" over what had happened at the Olympics but conceded he'd taken little notice of "Fentch" in LA and had little "flashback" of what "Rakovski" (Redzepovski) was like. Until he was told differently, he thought the world champion was a "little guy" who only came up to his chin. The fact that Jeff Fenech was some two to three inches taller than McCrory clearly shocked the American.

But he said he was confident even if he didn't seem so sure. He said Fenech was easy to hit "because he just stands there in front of you" and that he had the best chance of anyone so far to beat the champion because he would not "run away like Coffee" and was not "over the hill" like Zaragoza.

McCrory said he would take Fenech to school and drop him off, but when asked how exactly he planned to do that, he had a firm "no comment". No tactics had yet been devised, he said, and he would have to dwell on the best plan to adopt for quite some time before the fight.

He may have had comparable boxing skills to Jerome Coffee, but as a public speaker, the Olympic gold medallist just wasn't in the same class.

McCrory was joined in Sydney by his brother Milton, his

trainer Taylor Smith, his business manager Prentiss Byrd, who did most of the talking for him, and by his sparring partner Hurley Snead, the sawn-off American bantamweight champion who was placed well above McCrory in the world ratings but was being forced to stand aside to make way for Olympic Revenge. Two days before the fight, McCrory's mentor Emmanuel Steward came to town to oversee the challenger's final preparations.

Steward created the legend of the Kronk Gym. He turned a Detroit recreational centre into such a great nurturing ground for boxing talent that between 1978 and 1986 Kronk fighters would earn more than $30 million from the ring. Most of the money went to Steward's most famous and feared creation Thomas Hearns, the Motor City Hit Man, who became one of sport's great moneymakers with Super Fights against Sugar Ray Leonard, Marvelous Marvin Hagler, Roberto Duran and Wilfred Benitez.

A round-faced, youthful, black man, Steward made himself one of the most successful and powerful men in the cut-throat American boxing industry. He was in charge of 30 world class professionals and 70 amateurs with high hopes and the probability of success. Twelve lieutenants worked with him, turning talent into dollars and ring sense.

McCrory-Fenech was to be the 33rd world title bout featuring Kronk boxers.

Steward had a lofty opinion of Fenech. He called him a "real strong fighter" capable of beating WBA bantamweight champion Bernardo Pinango and his WBC counterpart Happy Lora, the conqueror of Daniel Zaragoza. But he was quick to claim that McCrory had the perfect style to score an early knockout.

Although McCrory had made a career of fighting veritable no-names, he said, those unknown opponents had often been tough, hardened club fighters who had taught McCrory to cope with a variety of different styles and situations. Had he wanted to, Steward said, he could easily have found matches for his man against has-beens like Zaragoza or runners like Coffee, but what would have been the point? Against obscure but dangerous club fighters, McCrory had been brought along the hard way. Just the sort of preparation he needed to beat a durable, strong, aggressive champion like Fenech. At least that's what Steward said.

"Fenech is easily the best of the bantamweight champions," Steward conceded. "But Steve is so terribly experienced. He has a tremendous background in boxing. I've seen him grow from a nine-year-old kid into an Olympic champion and now a world title challenger. He has the background, the speed and especially the motivation to beat Jeff Fenech. He deserves recognition and respect and as the first Olympic gold medallist to win a world pro title from the class of '84, he will become an immediate hero back in the States."

Steward was well versed in the art of teaching boxing and he also knew more tricks than his 100 fighters put together. After McCrory's surprisingly strong showing against Fenech, John Lewis would claim that he had been furnished with a tape of McCrory fighting Kenny Butts only because it deliberately exposed flaws in the gold medallist's style. Lewis believes it was Steward's intention to lull the Australian camp into a false sense of security.

"I reckon they said to one another over in Detroit: 'Let's send the one of Butts to those suckers down there and give 'em a helluva surprise'," Lewis claimed after the fight, "McCrory was a totally different fighter against Jeff than he had been on the videotape we were sent. But in the end they were the ones who were surprised. Jeff was more than equal to the task."

Steward tried to bait Fenech. On the eve of the title fight he labelled Fenech a "dirty fighter" and castigated Paul Moore for allowing Fenech to "get away with murder" against Zaragoza. He threatened terrible retribution if McCrory was subjected to the Fenech head-butt, shoulder-charge and swinging elbow.

At the weigh-in only hours before they would step into the ring, Steward claimed Fenech had been "held up" on the scales, a trick as old as weight limits themselves and one Steward was familiar with because, as he admitted, he had done it himself with other Kronk fighters.

As Fenech jumped on and off the scales and then started chomping into a plate of his mother's ravioli, Steward roared that someone next to the champion had placed a foot under the platform to make the scales register a weight below the true figure. Knowing of the well-publicised weight problems Fenech had endured leading up to the title fight, Steward was doing his best to compound the damage to Fenech's emotional state after weeks of savage dieting. Steward said there had been far too many people near the champion as he weighed

in, that the crush of television cameras and newspaper pho-
tographers had prevented him from properly witnessing the
champion's weight.

There is no doubt Fenech considered the benefits of trying
to cheat the scales while he was struggling to fit his body into
the confines of 118 pounds. But a secret trial weigh-in, held
while Steward and McCrory were still asleep that morning,
assured him he would make the bantamweight limit simply by
taking off his underpants. Fenech weighed in at the official
ceremony naked, but was on and off so quickly that Steward
and Prentiss Byrd were screaming interference. Steward demanded that John Lewis make Fenech get back on the scales.
Lewis told Steward to come and kiss him some place un-
pleasant. Chastened that his best Detroit stings had failed to
affect Fenech's trainer, Steward realised his prime chance of
making Steve McCrory the IBF bantamweight champion had
gone out the window faster than Mrs Fenech's ravioli down
her son's throat.

Fenech knew he had beaten McCrory the instant he made
118 pounds. The struggle to make the bantamweight limit for
the last time in his life had been the most trying part of the
McCrory campaign, the part which gave Fenech and Lewis
the most concern.

With a hand free of treachery and with his weight under
control, Fenech would almost certainly have ended Olympic
Revenge long before round 14. But because the swelling in his
fists flared every time he donned his training gloves, he was
unable to adequately prepare himself for the fight. Because of
the lack of fruitful time in the gymnasium, his weight reduc-
tion, a carefully monitored chore in his 13 previous fights,
was hampered.

"It was bloody sad watching Jeff trying to train for the
McCrory fight," Lewis recalls. "He was in the gym trying to
act as if there was nothing at all wrong with him. But he was
going through agony everytime he threw a punch. From the
time he beat Zaragoza, Jeff was only able to give a fraction of
himself. In the end he was trying to train with one hand, sparring blokes like Shane Knox and only using his right. He took
more punches in those sparring sessions that in all his other
fights put together. If I hadn't been so confident of Jeff's
chances, even with his preparation cut back, I would have
called the fight off a third time. Even if it meant Jeff giving up
the world title."

The chance to beat McCrory after two years of dreaming about it every other night, after two years of beating everyone put before him to create just such an opportunity, was too great a spur for Fenech to let McCrory get away a second time. Even if he had a bad hand there was, at least, no jury this time. Fenech wore special padding inside his training gloves that made the pain only a little less excruciating; he went to an executive fat farm to fast, and whenever his hand allowed, he trained with an intensity that went beyond even the most rigorous standards he had previously set. Once again he adopted the same aura of disquiet that had so unsettled Lewis before the rematch with Joey Glover back in the days when Fenech was a lillywhite amateur with the blackest of hearts.

With a digestive system malfunctioning because of his constant mix of laxatives and starvation, Fenech pressed on, relentlessly. Once in twilight training at Lewis' holiday home near Gosford on the NSW Central Coast, Fenech even soiled his pants while shadow boxing. It wasn't the first time diarrhoea had struck him in the middle of a training session and he did what he has always done under similar circumstances. He kept training. Punching away for another hour, despite the embarrassment and the discomfort.

He complained that he felt like a "filthy dog", but after going to the trainer's holiday home to escape the pressures of being a world champion, his personal fight with a drastic weight problem, a stomach disorder which flared at the most inconvenient times and a temper he was still trying hard to master, Fenech was prepared to feel like an animal if it meant he could train hard. He was ready to fight like an animal, too.

On the morning of the long-awaited big fight, he checked himself on the scales Mordey had given him as a 21st birthday present a year earlier. All through a sleepless night, after several hours spent wasting in the sauna, Fenech had been sweating it out, praying that, somehow, his excess poundage would disappear by morning, that, somehow, his metabolism and his determination would gang up on the unwanted kilos. And all night long, try as he might to dispel the notions from a mind already overflowing with dilemmas, Fenech couldn't help but brood about the fate of the last great bantamweight champion Richie Sandoval. The little American, who had topped Coffee in the 1980 US Olympic trials, had lost his WBA championship and almost lost his life against Gaby Canizales four months before Fenech would kill the title aspirations of McCrory. Sandoval was bounced off the canvas so often that when he hit the deck for the last time many ringsiders in Las Vegas thought he was dead. Sandoval's dramatic loss of form was blamed on his dramatic loss of weight.

When Fenech climbed from his bed at 4.30am on fight day and went through the ritual he had been dreading all through the hours he should have been asleep, he found he was four pounds overweight. Perfect, if he were challenging for his second world championship, the super-bantamweight title, but horrifying considering that McCrory, who already had the gold medal Fenech so dearly wanted, was looking a much better bet of stealing Fenech's bantamweight crown as well. Surely after two years waiting to get square, the unthinkable couldn't happen. Or could it? Could the champion's worst fears become reality? After two years of telling the whole country how he could have belted McCrory's gold medal right off if he'd been given the chance, would the smug little Olympic champion prove Fenech to be nothing more than an imposter and a dreamer?

"There was no way I could let him beat me because of the weight," Fenech remembers. "If McCrory was going to get my title as well as the gold medal, I was determined that he would have to beat me on ability and nothing else. No matter how weak it made me, I just had to make eight stone six and enter the ring as champion. I knew making the weight would be the hardest part of the fight, no matter what McCrory did once the bell went.

"Three days before the fight I was nine pounds overweight but I sweated a lot of it off and went without food until it almost drove me round the bend. But I was still too heavy on the morning of the fight. So, even though Lewie would never have allowed me if he'd been there, I put on three tracksuits and went for a run around Erskineville before it got light. I was probably out on the streets for an hour. When I came home I put the electric heater on and until John came to pick me up for the trial weigh-in at eight o'clock, I spent almost the whole time shadow boxing in front of that heater. I was terribly faint. I felt so bad I was sweating just thinking about what I was doing to my body. But eventually I made the weight and I made it all worthwhile."

Fenech was so gaunt, his face so hollow and grey, that when Lewis first laid eyes upon him that championship morning, tears sprung to his eyes. He wanted to stop the bout going ahead. He felt he had betrayed his friend by not calling it off sooner.

"But it was destiny," Fenech said, "For two years McCrory and I had been on a collision course. I couldn't stop now, no matter how Johnny felt. I promised I'd go out there and do some business on him."

Triumph did not come easily. In the sixth round Fenech's whole career flashed before his eyes and for a few brief, but debilitating seconds, Lewis feared the end of the line had arrived for them both. In a way they both feared but seldom admitted.

For the initial five rounds of the fight, Fenech, ever conscious of conserving what remained of his strength after his early morning exercises, outboxed McCrory with a jab painful to both. But in round six the aura of invincibility Fenech had created for himself and which he was doing his best to preserve, suddenly came unstuck. For the first time it looked like Fenech might be knocked out. For the one and only time, it looked like Emmanuel Steward's prediction was coming true. Fenech was headed for the canvas. Suddenly McCrory had transformed himself, with a single punch, a short left hook, into what Steward said he would become, the crisper puncher, the more polished executioner. McCrory came up with the hook on Fenech's usually guarded chin as the pair finished a torrid exchange late in the round. With that one punch McCrory changed the whole nature of the fight, and until his march to the title was stifled a few minutes later, he became infinitely more terrifying than a 22-year-old ex-amateur star with 11 so-so wins in 12 fights for money.

Suddenly he had done what Coffee and Zaragoza had been unable to do.

"No! No! He's gone! He's gone!" Lewis bellowed to Newtown team-mates in the corner. "I'm tellin' ya Jeff's shot."

It wasn't that McCrory's short left hook had been such a lethal punch, but for some reason, perhaps the shock that McCrory carried more sting than he expected, Fenech simply stopped fighting. He was stunned. Utterly. His eyes suddenly lost the malevolent stare with which he had loaded them minutes earlier. He was in the same position from where most of his victims succumbed. Backed up in a corner and under heavy fire. Suddenly in a Jeff Fenech fight, Jeff Fenech wasn't throwing punches.

Maybe if McCrory owned a bigger punch or greater tenacity or just a dab more killer instinct, the Fenech saga might have ended in that pulse-quickening sixth round with Fenech departing as quickly as he arrived on the international front. He was weak and hurt and tired. When he got hit it hurt, when he hit back it hurt. The fellow in front of him, looking for one last punch to finish it, was holding all the aces.

After boasting of what he would do to McCrory and that gold medal if he ever got his hands on both, Fenech's promises of Olympic Revenge looked as hollow as a politician's pledges before election day. Instead of making McCrory pay for what happened in Los Angeles, Fenech was peering into the room where Muhammad Ali had seen the alligators with their trombones. The room between the hall of consciousness and the dark corridor of stupor. And everyone thought it was going to be an easy one.

Suddenly McCrory was seeing the headlines in the Detroit Free Press, suddenly he was on network TV verbally sparring with Joan Rivers. Suddenly he could see himself packing his things and moving them from Milton's mansion to one of his very own. His only problem was that Fenech could see it too.

"Jeff! Jeff! Are you all right, son?" Lewis demanded breathlessly. "Tell me if ya hurt. Tell me the truth."

As he sat in his corner in the 60 sanguine seconds between round six and seven, Fenech's clouded gaze began to clear and the hating stare returned, never wavering as he glared across the ring at Steward and McCrory. When he answered Lewis he was never so sure of himself.

"Are you hurt, Jeff?"

"Don't be stupid, Johnny!" It was all Fenech needed to say. Such is his refusal to concede anything to an opponent that after the fight, despite the welts and wounds, Fenech was prepared to argue with anyone who reckoned he'd lost the sixth to McCrory. He'd been hurt, he'd at least admit that, hurt just a little bit, but he said he had landed a lot more punches than the American during the three minutes of attrition.

Fenech used the seventh round, cut short because of a time-keeping error, to regather his senses. As his head cleared, McCrory's chances of capitalising on his one great punch of the fight evaporated along with his world title dream.

By round eight Fenech was back to his original fight plan. He was slipping inside, underneath and around McCrory's jab and pounding the challenger wherever he saw skin. Despite his weight problems he refused to show fatigue, perhaps because he feared it would only encourage another left hook on the chin. Although McCrory's ability to answer Fenech's punches with his own began to waver from round eight on, the American's courage never faltered.

In round 13 a series of wild, often mis-directed shots from Fenech, culminating in a right to the solar plexus, knocked most of the fight from McCrory and dropped him, exhausted and exasperated, to the floor. He was up quickly but no longer fighting to win the world bantamweight title. He was battling to see out the full 15 rounds.

With instructions from Lewis of "No head-butts — nuthin' stupid" Fenech charged from his corner at the start of the 14th to finish Olympic Revenge with a belated knockout. Paul Moore had warned Fenech about head-butting before the fight, but with McCrory tottering, Fenech's fists were good enough to do the job. As Fenech shoved and shunted him around the ring like a tackling dummy at football practice, it was obvious McCrory no longer had the strength even to "run like Coffee". Moore stopped it.

It was over. At last. McCrory lost on his feet, bravely, and Fenech kissed the bantamweights goodbye for good. He paraded around the ring with a pewter medal around his neck. Everyone thought McCrory had handed over the gold, but no such luck. It was only a token medal from Mordey to make up for the one Fenech had missed out on in Los Angeles, but somehow that pewter medal was just as precious.

"Steve would have beaten any other bantamweight in the world tonight," Prentiss Byrd said as soon as it was over, "But not Jeff Fenech. He is awesome. We have no excuses."

With a smashed left hand, a week-and-a-half of stomach disorders, coupled with malnutrition and against an opponent tougher and more talented than just about anyone in Australia gave him credit for, Fenech had shown for the first time that he could take it as well as dish it out.

Watching from ringside as the sixth round shaped up to be Fenech's last as world champion, Paul Fenech prayed for the boy who had given him so many rough times and then so many great ones. After the fight he could do nothing but marvel at the extraordinary fortitude of a kid who came back, when, for so many reasons, he should have called it quits.

"You know my boy is very, very brave," Paul Fenech said.

"I am very proud of him. Sometimes I think he must have two hearts. Maybe before he was born, God gave him some of mine."

Fenech put his performance down to something else. Not his heart but the brain of the man who had guided him from day one in the gym.

"I hope this proves to everyone that if Lewie had been with me in LA, I could have been the first Australian to win an Olympic gold medal in boxing," the winner and still champion said from the ring. "John Lewis is the greatest boxing trainer in the world. No contest. Without him I'd be in Long Bay Jail today."

The tears that gushed from Fenech in his dressingroom, once he was concealed from the public eye, would only be a trickle compared to the tears that would flow from the Fenech family in the weeks to follow.

Long Bay Jail claimed someone else. Godfrey Fenech. Awaiting trial for murder.■

19
A Second World Title

*"We should have known that Muhammad Ali
would not settle for any old resurrection. So
having rolled away the rock, he hit George
Foreman on the head with it"*
        Hugh McIlvanney, British writer.

They all said it would be a tough fight and a big risk for Fenech. His first bout in nine months, against the tough and ruthless Tony "Mad Dog" Miller, his old amateur enemy. It shaped up as a furious 12-rounder. At least most people thought it did. Everyone but those in the Fenech camp who told him differently.

Fenech was due to fight Samart Payakarun on March 13, 1987. It was to be his first fight since retaining his bantamweight title against Steve McCrory the previous July. No warm-up. No need.

But Samart was smart. He and his managers squeezed another $40,000 out of promoter Mordey. Then they postponed the fight, saying Samart had twisted his ankle. Fenech was shattered. After two major operations on his left fist and months of uncertainty over his future, it looked as though a big opportunity was to pass.

He was primed, like a keg of gunpowder, and Lewis wanted him to explode against someone, anyone, providing there was no risk of a backfire. He knew that if Fenech didn't have a fight soon he would go stale very quickly. Within days of Samart postponing his title defence against Fenech, who by now had relinquished his IBF world bantamweight title for bigger and more lucrative things, Fenech was matched with Miller for the English-born boxer's Australian featherweight title.

Mad Dog was tough. And just crazy enough to do anything to win. Since losing to Fenech as an amateur flyweight, he had been a slaughterman and a sparring partner for Lester Ellis and had won the featherweight title from the Melbourne veteran Paul Ferreri. He fought a draw with Antonio Rivera who had gone on to win the IBF featherweight title. And he had lost a close decision to Ellis in his last bout.

Barry Michael turned up to watch Fenech train for the fight at Jack Rennie's gym in Essendon, the same tiny gym in Melbourne's Marco Polo Street where Rennie's best-known pupil Lionel Rose had learned to be a world bantamweight champion. There existed an icy courtesy between Fenech and Michael, who because of the Sydney mauler's abdication, had become Australia's only world boxing champion at that time.

Fenech hadn't yet won two world titles, but he was already ticking over in his mind the concept of beating Michael for the IBF junior-lightweight crown, which together with the bantamweight and super-bantamweight titles and the world featherweight championship he expected to win at the end of 1987, would give him four world title belts. A first. Something the great Henry Armstrong and the mighty Roberto Duran could not accomplish.

Michael said he expected the Fenech-Miller fight to be "an absolute war". Two rough, strong, aggressive fighters, both well-versed in rule bending, locked together to see who would snap first.

Michael was wrong. There was no war. Just a revolting assault against an opponent who, due to courage or stupidity, never once thought about waving the white flag. Fenech put Miller on the canvas in the first round and pounded him for the remaining 11 to win a ludicrously lopsided decision. The Mauler was back. He had been resurrected from retirement.

Three times Miller's devoted trainer Brian Levier wanted to throw in the towel. Three times his fighter said no.

After the bout Fenech praised a warrior who "if run over by a bus on the way to the stadium, would still turn up to do his fans proud". Miller praised a fighter who carried a bus in his left fist and kept it in overdrive.

The fight marked even greater advances in professionalism for Fenech on his march to two world championships. Beforehand, Lewis had grave fears that the bout would degenerate into a head-butting duel when the action became most fierce. A case of who could come up with the dirtier tricks.

Before the fight Lewis gave Fenech a finger-waving lecture.

"Listen, Jeff," he said, their eyes meeting from six inches

away in the dressing room at the Melbourne Sports and Entertainment Centre, "If I see one head-butt or one deliberate low blow from you I'm heading straight home. You'll be coming back to an empty corner. All this business about you being a great street-fighter is terrific, but we're not on the streets now, we're on TV. If Miller wants to play rough let him go for his life and we'll wait for the referee to step in. No bloody head butts."

Fenech had used his head in more ways than one against Shingaki, Coffee, Zaragoza and McCrory and referee Denzil Creed, a controversial appointment to the Miller fight, told him there'd be nothing of that sort while he was the boss.

He said the same sort of thing to Miller who once knocked out the much-beaten Tiger Mann after first hitting him in the groin, then extending a hand of friendship before chopping down the unsuspecting victim with a blow to the chin.

Fenech hurt his left hand in the seventh round and his right hand in the ninth. After Miller had survived a fearful battering in the early rounds, Fenech decided to coast through the later rounds and avoid unnecessary risk to his fists. Samart was too precious to chance another hand operation.

Fenech's cruise to victory over Miller, devoid of any infringements and thus an indication of a growing professionalism, was an important gauge to assessing his chances of beating the Thai with the advantages in height, reach and power.

Fenech was getting the opportunity to do what no other Australian boxer had ever done. Such was the importance of the occasion that Lewis called in two of his oldest friends to help in Fenech's preparation for his 16th fight and the most important of his career. Charlie Gergen, who had trained Tony Mundine during the latter part of the great puncher's career, and Manny Hinton, an amateur trainer Lewis revered, both worked with Fenech for the title fight. They advised Lewis and boosted his confidence. They assured him of Fenech's capabilities, if, in fact, he ever really needed that assurance. They told him the things he wanted to hear. The things he knew were true but wanted to hear just the same.

Lewis devised basic strategies to beat a quality southpaw with a mallet punch. He had Fenech sparring with the "peek-a-boo" stance Cus D'Amato had used with Floyd Patterson, Jose Torres and Mike Tyson. So on the big night, with both fists on either side of his chin, Fenech was able to march straight into Samart, taking his biggest punches on his gloves and countering with thumping right crosses over Samart's right hand leads. His tight defence allowed him to rain blows on Samart's body and to use his physical strength to the greatest advantage.

Lewis also showed Fenech some wrestling moves to thwart Samart's attempts to clinch when Fenech elected to take the fight to the body. The strategy was to twist Samart's arms in close and if necessary, to break them.

The first time Samart and Fenech met was at the weigh-in at the Entertainment Centre, 10am on fight day May 8, 1987. Samart seemed drawn and nervous. Fenech confident, cocky and aggressive. Samart's manager Sombhop started snarling at Fenech: "You dead, you dead." Fenech hinted that Sombhop, said to have wagered $100,000 on Samart, would look pretty funny with his "head shoved up his arse". Sombhop took the hint and piped down.

In the ring on fight night, Sombhop was still telling Fenech that the Grim Reaper was coming, but the Australian was too psyched up to reply.

In his dressing room before the fight, surrounded by his handlers and old friends, Fenech made an emotional promise to the people who gave him strength.

"I just want youse all to know that I love each and everyone of youse and that I won't let any of youse down. You all mean the world to me."

Fenech had just finished reading a letter from Steve Mortimer, the former Australian rugby league half-back, who wrote of loyalty, mateship and the pursuit of excellence.

Lewis also thanked everyone in the room. He talked about determination. He described Fenech as the world's greatest living athlete. The best fighter pound for pound on earth. The rebirth of a young Duran.

The crowd in the cluttered change room then locked hands and the energy seemed to flow straight into Fenech's fists. Within minutes he was climbing through the ropes, ready to kill or be killed. Within 11 minutes and 42 seconds from the opening bell he was the new world super-bantamweight champion.

It is exciting stuff. It is never a close fight. Fenech is caught off balance by a pitty-pat right jab late in the first round when both his feet are off the canvas. He stumbles, hits the floor and is up before American referee Arthur Mercante, working his 74th world title fight, can start the count.

Officially it is recorded as a knockdown.

"Bullshit it was a knockdown," Fenech says later. "There was no power in the punch at all. He just caught me off-balance. I tripped over my own feet. My mum's hit me harder than that."

But officially, a knockdown it is. The first time, amateur or pro, he's been off his feet. Fenech loses the opening round by two points after having had Samart back-pedalling throughout. A lot of ground to make up.

"I just tried not to let it bother me," he says later. "I knew I had to stay calm and keep the fight plan fresh in my mind. I couldn't let being on the canvas rattle me. I just had to go out and win the next round. And the next and the next. Every round."

In the second, Samart hits Fenech with a ferocious uppercut. But the Aussie is already starting to catch up with the running champion. In the third, Fenech does what he does best. He starts to ruin another fighter's career. He traps Samart on the ropes and lets go. For a moment it looks like Mercante might stop it. But the bell rings and Samart lives to fight another round. In the fourth, Samart gives it everything he has — three, four left crosses, thrown so hard his whole body shudders from the force. But they hit glove and not chin. Late in the round Samart is trapped and gored by the bull he had planned on tormenting. A right cross takes his feet away and a sickening uppercut, while he's heading for the floor, makes sure he stays there.

For four minutes he is unconscious. He swallows his tongue, but Mercante, who did the same thing for Ingemar Johansson against Floyd Patterson more than a quarter of a century before, stops him from choking. Slowly, Samart is revived and lifted back to his feet and then to an ambulance. If he has taken a dive, as some claim, he has done a convincing job. For a while there are grave fears for his life.

Two world titles! The enormity of the feat can be gauged by the fact that very few boxers ever earn the right to fight for one.

And yet, in less than three years since turning professional Fenech has captured two world championships and has been hit by no more than 10 decent punches. By the end of 1987 he will have earned more than one million dollars. He has never been badly hurt. He has never been truly extended. He has defied the dangers of boxing and maximised the rewards to such an extent that, disregarding his hand injuries, he is totally free of scars. Boxing really has been good to him.

"Payakarun hit me with a great uppercut, McCrory hit me with a couple of good clean shots, Zaragoza landed a beauty in the sixth round but that's about it," Fenech says, his face broken by a huge smile at the realisation of his immense good fortune. Boxing is in a sport where people are supposed to get hurt and short-changed.

From a different perspective, he has shattered the careers of Ilesia Manila, Rolly Navarro, Satoshi Shingaki and John Farrell. And he has broken the spirit of Jerome Coffee, Steve McCrory and Samart Payakarun.

"It's crazy but it's true. I've won two world championships and I've never been hurt or been in trouble. Of course, I've been hit hard in a few sparring sessions, but there's no way the money I've made hasn't been worth it all."

As Samart was struggling to come to terms with the fact his prized title had been torn away, all kinds of presentations were being made in the ring after the dramatic finish.

One-time cleaning lady Mary Fenech was being presented with a fur coat. Arthur and Gloria Mercante received gifts for their 33rd wedding anniversary. Fenech was handing over $10,000 to charity. Samart was getting nothing but urgent medical attention.

The Marrickville Mauler was in his element, kissing and hugging the people in his corner and thanking a lot of people who had helped him. Grabbing the microphone he addressed the 12,000 fans who had roared with anticipation when he strutted his way into their presence and when he had Samart stuck helpless against the ropes.

"I love youse all," Fenech yelled to the crowd. "With 12,000 of the most beautifullest people in the world cheering me on, it's hard to feel pain. I know youse paid to see me and there's no way in the world I'd let youse all down. Thank you all very much."

Fenech had fractured the English language, but more to the point, he had broken another fighter's heart.

The next day a public relations company offered Fenech some free advice about speech-making.

"I don't need no elocution lessons," he told them. "The people love me because I'm Jeff Fenech." ■

20
Life And Death

*"Defeat is worse than death, because you have
to live with defeat"*

Bill Musselman,
Minnesota basketball coach, 1972.

In the weeks after the crowning achievement of his life to
that time and after several weeks of training in almost
monastic austerity, it was party time for Jeff Fenech. He pre-
yed at every nightclub and disco between Sydney's eastern
suburbs and the resorts of Queensland's Barrier Reef.

His popularity was at an all-time high. He knew it. And he
made the most of the good times.

Samart Payakarun, the fighter whose prone body Fenech
had stepped over to bask in the bright lights, also prayed. But
his monastic austerity was of a different kind. Buddist monas-
ticism. Shaven skull, saffron robes, penance, shame and re-
gret. And fear.

Early in April, 1987 when Payakarun left Bangkok where
he had earned a reputation for being a bit of a devil in the
City of Angels, the World Boxing Council super-
bantamweight champion was feted as a conquering hero off to
war in Australia. He left the country as its most notorious sex
symbol and playboy, Thailand's most celebrated sporting
hero.

At the age of 24, Samart had lived for a long time in the
spotlight. As a champion in Thai fighting, the lethal art of
kick-boxing peculiar to his country, Samart had been a
wealthy Thai idol for several years before he out-boxed former world junior-flyweight champion Netroi Vorasingh in
his first professional fight under the rules set down by the
Marquess of Queensberry. He had learned to love the attention and the adoration, especially from a select group of
sultry nightclub singers who were often romantically linked

with the part-time male model and stylish southpaw.

On May 10, Samart arrived back in Bangkok without the WBC title belt he had worn so proudly. What he did have was a whole lot of new enemies.

There had been grave fears for Samart's life when Fenech crumpled the sleek, slim Thai late in the fourth round of their championship bout. The 12,000 packed into the Entertainment Centre and the 50 million television viewers had seen one of the world's best boxers smashed into some senseless cadaver by Fenech in a little under 12 minutes.

But as they were loading him into the back of an ambulance bound for nearby St Vincent's Hospital immediately after the carnage and crowning of a new king, Samart's life wasn't the only one at risk.

As he toppled helpless towards the four ropes and then went down as Fenech finished him off with a right cross and an uppercut to the side of an already spinning head, a death warrant was already being signed for the fallen idol back home.

Rumours that Samart had been paid to lose spread like hunger pangs in a Bangkok prison. Before 24 hours had passed, almost all of Thailand had been convinced their hero was nothing more than a boozing, womanising fraud who put his pocket before national honour.

The beaten champion denied the charges vehemently. But he had few believers.

"I did nothing dishonourable," Samart told reporters after the fight. "I underestimated Fenech. I did not train hard enough. He was very strong and a much harder puncher than I thought. I will give up my playboy lifestyle and concentrate on training, I have made a mistake and I will never repeat that mistake."

Samart arrived home at Bangkok airport in disgrace.

The beautiful women said to have hampered his preparation for the fight, were not there to welcome him.

Instead, there were police reinforcements holding back angry mobs of hecklers while airport workers surrounded the handsome anti-hero, enveloped him in abuse and demanded to know the size of the bribe which had enticed him into such a shameful capitulation.

There were even farmers from his hometown in Cholburi province to give him a serve. Samart soon learnt that a group of furious Thai gamblers had paid a contract killer $600 to release their venom into a single shot between the disgraced fighter's dark, brooding eyes. At least three people died in the few days after the Sydney disaster.

One of Bangkok's leading boxing promoters, Mana-ong-Saengkul was shot dead by four gunmen while he sat in the back of his chauffeur-driven BMW. Another Thai committed suicide after he lost all his money backing his hero. A third man was shot dead after refusing to pay 20 of his neighbours who had backed the Marrickville Mauler at the surprisingly long odds of 3-1.

No wonder Samart looked so uneasy puffing on a cigarette before boarding the flight home from Sydney, showing no outward signs of battle, but bearing emotional scars that would be torn raw when he arrived home to a villain's reception. His decision to enter the monastry at Cholburi province, an hour's drive south-east of Bangkok, came during the most traumatic period of his life. Rarely has the gulf between victor and vanquished been so gaping. While Fenech was being feted as Australia's greatest ever boxer and the only one to win two world titles, Samart was undergoing a self-imposed purge of all the negativity in his soul. It is not uncommon for young Thai men to enter a monastry for a short time during their lives. Usually the induction comes after some great personal grief.

Certainly the sight of Samart without his thick, dark hair and with flowing robes replacing the sartorial trappings his celebrity status demanded, must have been something of a shock to those who had worshipped him as the sporting god of Thailand. Samart's entry into a life without women or alcohol, of begging for food and with lots of "meditatin' and prayin'", as Muhammad Ali had so often referred to his Muslim obligations, was seen by many as a way of saving face with a country which had turned on him. Perhaps it was even a way of saving his life, hiding out until tempers cooled and the guns of the hired killers were holstered.

While Samart busied himself with prayers, one eye always looking over his shoulder, reporters, experts and critics searched for reasons to explain how the man who looked so magical beating up Lupe Pintor and Juan Meza, could produce no spell against a little-known Aussie.

The media also conducted stake-outs on just about every nightclub singer in Bangkok's Thomburi district, where Samart was said to be more famous for his performances outside the boxing ring. A restaurant singer named Ni, said to have become Samart's lover after the failure of an earlier romance and another singer named Sompong, with whom Samart sometimes strayed and stayed, were targeted for blame over their man's defeat. A third female admirer was rarely off the telephone to Samart who spent $500 a week in calls while staying in Sydney.

As Fenech soaked up the sun on Great Keppel Island off the Queensland coast after his historic and unique win, his victim soaked up more punishment than he had been forced to endure during the worst beating of his life.

The simple and most honest explanation for Samart's demise was that he struck an absolute fighting freak in Fenech. Samart had the punching power to knock out anyone and he had the boxing skills to jab, slip, slide and dance his way to victory for 12 rounds.

But faced with an opponent whose defensive tactics were almost contemptuous and who was constantly pressing forward, hurling a steady stream of damaging punches, Samart simply caved in under the pressure. The signs of such a demise had been there for months. Ever since Fenech and Lewis had watched a tape of Samart knocking out the once-mighty, but then washed-up, Lupe Pintor to win the WBC title, they had been convinced that Fenech's pressure and strength would prove too much.

"See how he always holds when Pintor gets close," Fenech would tell Lewis, "See how when Pintor starts throwing punches Payakarun jumps away. I'll stay in his face all the time and make him fight." Lewis nodded.

Their analysis of Samart's style proved accurate in Samart's first title defence against Meza, the fighter Pintor beat to win the title. That fight in December, 1986 was little more than a sparring session for Samart who toyed with and mocked Meza for 11 rounds. At times, he made the once proud world champion look amateurish, and then pulled down the shutters with a single left cross in the 12th round. The performance was little short of awesome. But the flaws, however minute, in Samart's repertoire, flashed like airport beacons to Fenech and Lewis.

The handwriting for Samart's downfall had also been on the wall of John McColl's Glebe Estate Gym, where Samart spent a month training for the Fenech fight. Sure enough he showed the flashes of brilliance that separated him from just another stinging puncher. He made his sparring partners Downmai Sithkodom and Thongberm Vongvianyai miss outrageously and wobbled them occasionally with the axe he carried in his left fist. But despite the pirouettes, the sharp shuffles away from punches, the bobbing and weaving, the swivelling of a neck that seemed made of rubber and the frequent glances into the mirror to see how he was looking, Samart simply did not train with the manic-intensity of Fenech in full flight.

It was as though, so sure of victory, he wanted more to entertain the on-lookers than prepare for a battle with a demon. He was, however, training harder than in March when the Fenech fight was originally scheduled but was postponed because it was claimed Samart had twisted an ankle. The real reason was more likely that Samart simply was in such poor condition that his handlers felt he would have no chance against Fenech. Two months later he still had no chance.

But the Bangkok dailies were full of other theories for the sad demise. The two most popular items of speculation were that Samart's girlfriend was a heavy gambler who persuaded him to throw the fight and clean up with the bookies or that after announcing plans to move to Sydney after the fight, Samart had taken a $100,000 bribe on top of his $250,000 purse to make life Down Under just that little more comfortable.

Everybody it seemed, put the boxing boot into Samart when he was down. His manager Sombhop turned his back on him. Thailand's Prime Minister General Prem Tinsulanonda, who looked so pleased the night Samart tortured Juan Meza, was aghast by what was seen in political circles as a serious blow to national pride, and twice telephoned Samart at the Koala Motor Inn in Sydney's Oxford Square, to vent his anger.

No one, it seemed, had a good word for Samart. Even Charlie Atkinson, the hard as nails English trainer who worked with several other world champs before walking out on Samart in Bangkok, admitted the previously unbeaten champion could sometimes be a playboy and a fool.

Atkinson quit as Samart's trainer five weeks before the Fenech fight because he was frustrated by his champion's greater fondness for alcohol and women than for the disciplines of professional boxing. He told Samart's other handlers to take their boy to Australia as soon as possible so he would be rid of the temptations of Thomburi and the Pattaya resort where he usually trained and where he had bought his parents a prawn exporting business. Two days before the fight Atkinson was summoned to Sydney to work in the corner as cut man, interpreter and trouble-shooter when the Thais began to have doubts about their man's chances.

Atkinson, who had worked with world champs like John Conteh, Azumah Nelson and another Thai, Sot Chitalada, described suggestions that Samart threw the fight as "ludicrous".

"For Thais, there is such a thing as honour," he said. "To throw a fight would amount to a death sentence in Bangkok. I've had my differences with Samart, but I know he would never throw a fight. Although he has committed many sins, it appears he may well have been more sinned against. I believe he was given some terrible advice."

Certainly if Samart planned to take a dive, he could have taken an easier route than to stand up against Fenech and a spate of viciousness that could have caused permanent damage.

Samart claimed bad advice had contributed to his downfall along with diuretic tablets and the sudden, necessary loss of 10kg. He made a great many excuses, but when he met Fenech and Lewis after the fight in the hotel room he had called home for a month, he summed up his loss succinctly.

"You very strong," he told Fenech, a little embarrassed by his failure to mount much of a serious title defence. "You very strong."

Lewis told Samart his champion had won the fight for all of Australia.

Samart's assistant manager Yingyong Parnichphol, a small smiling man who had images of Buddha dangling from his neck, listened closely. He had other ideas.

Pointing at Lewis and smiling broadly, Yingyong said: "No. No. Not just for Australia. No. No. He win for you. He win for you, Mr Lewis. He win for you." ■

21
Flying High

He was somewhere between Honolulu, Hawaii and
Denver, Colorado, poised six miles above the Pacific
Ocean, when he began to outline details about the aura of im-
mortality he had created in his own mind.

The long, narrow cut under his right eye was starting to
heal and as the sun began to struggle above the horizon, the
reality was starting to dawn on Jeff Fenech that for four
rounds he had knocked down and tortured King Carlos
Zarate, a name to quicken the heart and stir the soul of boxing aficionados.

But bound for London to see Joe Bugner's last comeback
end in despair, Fenech was more concerned about preserving
his own life than reflecting on the fact he had helped mangle
the legend of one of the greatest fistfighters ever to escape a
Mexican slum.

"Ya reckon if this fell out of the sky would we all get blown
up or just drown?" he asked, making sure the query was loud
enough to raise the pulses of his fellow passengers.

"Would it burst into flames or just break into little pieces?"

He gave a betraying laugh, mindful that he was gaining a
nervous, and all-too captive audience.

"Anyway I know one thing. Everyone else could do their
best, but I'd end up swimming to England. I've always had a
special feeling about me. I've always believed that even if bad
things happen around me, I can live through them. I'm a sur-
vivor.

"It's a feeling like — I don't know — like I'm invincible.
Don't ask me why, but for my whole life I've always thought I

was a little bit blessed."

He was only kidding a little.

Throughout his life Jeff Fenech, the most successful fighter in Australia's 200-year history, has always triumphed over adversity.

It was late in October, 1987. He was giving trans-Pacific passengers a detailed description of what happens when a Jumbo jet crashes and clearly revelling in the belief that he was impervious to disaster.

High in the sky and high on life, he was a two-time world champion gunning for title number three, having just beaten one of the all-time greats, even if his eye was cut along the way.

Lewis sat next to him, enjoying the way Fenech's good natured banter made the other people on the aircraft look sideways out the window.

How circumstances change.

Just three years earlier Fenech had also been poised six miles above the Pacific Ocean. That time he was going the other way. Alone. And angry. And frustrated and hurt. His world had crashed around him in a screaming, tearful heap.

Fenech had flown home from Los Angeles despondent and disillusioned, the dream he shared with Lewis of an Olympic gold medal, taken from him by a cruel miscarriage of justice. He had vowed to get even. With a voice choked by sobs he had told anyone prepared to listen that he'd show those senile old men, as he called them. He'd show them what kind of fighter Jeff Fenech was. And now six miles above the Pacific, he felt secure in the knowledge that he had kept his bargain. He had shown the world. And those senile old men, in particular.

Fenech beat Carlos Zarate by a technical decision at the end of the fourth round of their one-sided fight at the Hordern Pavilion on October 16. He caught the Jumbo jet to London two days later, his head still dizzy from celebrations and his face still bandaged from Zarate's head-butt.

Fenech had knocked the aged Mexican down and was on his way to certain knockout victory when the wise old warrior tried the one last option open to him. He rammed his balding head into Fenech's cheekbone, opening a five centimetre wound. It was the end of the fight, if you could call their meeting such. It was more like a boy finding an old man walking home late at night, then mugging him and stealing his dignity. Fenech, so far ahead on points that you wondered how

Zarate was still standing, was declared the winner.

As Hugh McIlvanney, the English sportswriter, once said, "Money talks, but in boxing blood usually has the last word."

Victory over the old man further cemented Fenech's place in boxing history. By the end of 1987 he was one of the most recognisable of Australians. He was a millionaire who had risen from the gutter. The hating, animalistic snarl that terrified other street kids had proved just as successful against world boxing champions. Fenech used to bash people up when there wasn't much to watch on TV. Now he was getting paid to bash people up while others watched *on* TV — to pay for his fast cars, plush houses and flash wardrobe.

Zarate really had no chance of beating Fenech, even if head butts had been allowed under the rules of professional boxing. Fenech refused to be intimidated by Zarate's record, which was among the best in boxing history. He walked through the old king's body shots as though they were slaps. He sent Zarate home to his furniture store in Mexico City, a badly beaten loser. Five months later Zarate would be stopped in 10 rounds by Daniel Zaragoza for the WBC super-bantamweight title, Fenech would vacate.

In his youth Fenech was nothing more than a sneak, sometimes a liar and petty thief.

But this is the same fellow who a few years later on the afternoon of his historic punch-up with Samart Payakarun, would accept the well wishes of the Australia Prime Minister, while stirring a saucepan full of pre-fight porridge.

"Yeah thanks very much, Bob," he had said on the phone. "Thanks for the call, mate. I won't let nobody down."

This is the same fellow who on July 10, 1987, victimised the American super-bantamweight champion, Greg "The Flea" Richardson, only days after his brother Godfrey had been sent to prison for life following a grisly murder and only days after Fenech's father Paul had almost died for the umpteenth time during a turbulent life of ill-health.

Fenech's mother agonises over her son every time he fights, just as his father had done when he was alive. Yet the fighter relishes the conflict like little else in his life.

He ponders only occasionally on the consequences. Death and brain damage, the harsh facts that doctors use as ammunition in an on-going assault on boxing, are subjects he dismisses with a shrug of the shoulders.

The safety measures in boxing are adequate, he says. "It's

safer than football, motor racing, hang gliding."

And anyway he had John Lewis in his corner. His protector. Together they had breathed new life into the fight game and extended the 15 minutes of fame Andy Warhol allotted to everyone on the planet, into a good few years.

Boxing has been an eternal fascination. Love or despise it, the sight of men fighting arouses interest among great masses of people. When Fenech was a boy nothing made him such an instant celebrity as the fact he could pound any other kid's face into a bloody mush.

There is something so primeval, pre-historic and basic about boxing. It arouses latent hostility in just about anyone who watches.

The sight of grown men fighting like prize roosters for the entertainment of others. The great champions going off to battle for their people. By October, 1987, Fenech had managed to make his conquests pay handsomely. He bought cars for his family, homes for himself at Erskineville, Gosford and a new mansion at Five Dock and he made the whole of Australia sit up and take notice of a gutsy kid, who in the boxing ring, was so much more than a dead-end no-hoper.

Boxing could never reform him totally. His anger still frightens him. Sometimes the thought of what he might do to someone when he snaps, scares him awake at night. "It's hard to keep the fire under control," he once told journalist Winsor Dobbin. "Sometimes my intensity really scares me. I think that one day I'm going to blow up."

But depsite the enormity of his achievements, despite his wealth and fame, his charismatic hold on a large section of Australia's sporting public, Fenech remains largely unchanged from the laughing, joking prankster who endeared himself to the inner sanctum of friends that surrounds his life and career.

He has no specific ambition apart from winning four, perhaps five, world boxing titles and maybe one day returning to the sport he first showed promise in, rugby league, whether it be as a coach or player.

A few years before, his great dream was to be a first grade rugby league player. By the time he beat Zarate, Fenech was an international celebrity in something George Foreman once called "the sport to which all other sports aspire".

And he had become so adept at the business level of boxing that he was negotiating his own six-figure purses with Bill

Mordey and piecing together sponsorships of similar amounts from the Reebok shoes and Durant food companies.

For most of his career Fenech has been a boxing champion who beat opponents with deformed fists and who called upon seemingly boundless reserves of stamina even though he was unable to breathe through a nose repeatedly broken from a footballing adolescence.

Shortly after he beat Samart Payakarun, Fenech told Janet Hawley of *The Age* Melbourne: "No I don't want to learn nothing. I'm happy being who I am. I'm not interested in books. I've read two books on the history of boxing, I think. I don't want to work or run a business.

"All I want to do is do what I'm doing now — hang around with my mates, train, play sport, then get married and have some kids and spoil them and spoil my family. I owe my mum and dad a lot and I know now they tried to teach me the right things.

"I'll stay in boxing for as long as I like it — it might be another six months or six years or I might get knocked out in my next fight and it could be the end.

"I never was a person to think far ahead. I live day by day. When I wake up in the morning, I just hope I'm going to be here again tomorrow." ■

22
Three Times a Champ

"Oh yeah. I like the pressure, need the pressure. People like to see underdogs that do it. People like to be there when history is made."

Muhammad Ali.

"This is heaven on earth," sighed Jeff Fenech as he lay on his electrically controlled bed, waited for his spa bath to fill with water just the right temperature and gazed longingly and lovingly at the Pacific breakers crashing on a kilometre of sun-drenched golden sand.

Fenech knew it was exactly a kilometre because his years of roadwork made him an expert on distances. And every morning he ran that beach with his mates while the waves came in and the girls came down to sunbake.

Paradise never looked so good.

It costs a lot of money to stay at the Aanuka Beach Resort at Coffs Harbour, the banana capital of Australia and a sunny tourist mecca on the Pacific Highway between Sydney and Brisbane.

A few years before it would have taken a few of his dad's weekly pension cheques just to pay for a day's accommodation in the pastel-coloured, Ken Done-decorated resort suites that make life luxury for the honeymooners, merchant bankers and world famous fist-fighters who stay there.

But in the last days of February, 1988, when autumn had taken just enough sting from the coastal sun, the people at Aanuka Beach were paying Jeff Fenech to stay there with 10 of his mates — an assortment of friends, tacticians, a trainer and sparring partners.

And not only was the resort paying Fenech for the patronage, but it was turning a holiday resort into a complete Fenech training camp, building a sparring ring in a function room, setting up punching bags, ferrying in groupies and even turning over the keys of the resort's red Ferrari for trips into town.

This is what being the champion of the world means to Jeff Fenech in a tangible sense. Adulation and respect are great. But better still are money and good times he would not have known even if he had become the finest rugby league player ever to wear shoulder pads and a cauliflower ear.

Fenech spent eight days in Coffs Harbour training for his March 7 fight with vicious Victor Callejas, a 27-year-old Puerto Rican of extreme arrogance and immense punching power who had not been beaten in a professional fist fight since the previous decade. That loss was the only time Callejas had ever been beaten inside the ropes. He boasted of having never lost outside them on the street.

Callejas liked wearing his reflective sunglasses and chewing matchsticks. He scoffed and spat in disgust whenever Fenech's name cropped up in conversation.

But despite Callejas' great record, his big punch, his 20 quick knockouts in 23 fights, and the confidence matched only by that of the immovable force he was fighting, the Fenech-Callejas battle for the WBC featherweight championship quickly developed into a one-sided, one-handed, one-way bout. Fenech did all the throwing and Callejas did all the catching.

Fenech gave Callejas a terrible beating in a spiteful, dirty fight in which both boxers used their heads as auxiliary weapons to their fists and in which Fenech was frequently assaulted by the Puerto Rican's well-aimed elbows and deadly accurate thumb.

In beating Callejas, Fenech joined the likes of Henry Armstrong, Barney Ross, Bob Fitzsimmons, Sugar Ray Leonard and Thomas Hearns as only one of 11 fighters in boxing history to hold three world crowns. Soon he would go gunning to match the four championships compiled by Hearns, Detroit's "Motor City Hit Man", a few months before.

Fenech stopped Callejas in the 10th round of their 12-round fight for the title vacated by the long-time champ Azumah Nelson, who had moved up to the WBC junior-lightweight title and an inevitable big-bucks fight with the Australian. In winning the championship Fenech won back the title which had meandered around the world from the time a seemingly-uninspired Johnny Famechon had lost it to Vincente Saldivar.

Fenech beat Callejas exactly as he and John Lewis had conspired when they sat down together in Coffs Harbour to work out tactics, risks, counter-punches and chances. In the first round Callejas landed his most dangerous punch, a left uppercut-cum-hook of the type which once lifted the Italian world champ Loris Stecca off his feet and sent him crashing to the canvas with a broken jaw.

The left hook was a "real beauty" Fenech would later admit and it momentarily stunned the young man on his way to history. But Fenech answered it with the same arrogance with which it had been thrown. He merely dropped his hands and looked deadpan into Callejas piercing black eyes.

Vicious Victor was beaten from that moment on. But in what would be the dirtiest, most spiteful and best fight of Fenech's career, the Puerto-Rican had to endure a plethora of painful assaults until round 10, surviving two knockdowns and a one-handed barrage from Fenech which would have left all but the lead-headed unconscious.

Instead, Callejas lost on his feet with the kind of misguided dignity that Latin-American warriors pride themselves upon. He was beaten until he was left reeling around the ring in such a pathetic condition that American Richard Steele, a referee who had once stopped Marvin Hagler from eating Thomas Hearns, called an early finish.

Steele admitted he could have stopped it a little sooner, but Victor was a proud fighter who wanted to go out on his shield, even if he risked going out in a coffin instead.

Victor Callejas was also a pretty nasty piece of work. The former WBA super-bantamweight champion, who had been forced to relinquish the championship because of a feud with his manager Pepe Cordero, tried every dirty trick in the book to stop Fenech's punches from constantly raking his head and body.

"He's head-butted me a hundred times," Fenech screamed at Steele between rounds seven and eight. "He's been elbowing me all night and just then he stuck his thumb right down into my eye socket."

Callejas started the fight as the aggressor. But for most of the fight the hunter was the hunted and his prey was a relentless predator seemingly impervious to pain or doubt.

After the fight, in which Callejas spent a lot of time back-pedalling and spitting blood from a cut mouth, the beaten bomber called Fenech a great champion and sent congratulations from his dressing room. He wasn't about to apologise, mind you, just give credit where credit was due.

"——————————— him," snarled Fenech, "I'll take him outside and kill 'im now." Fenech had a lot of reasons to be a sore winner.

Both his eyes were closing from the Callejas head-butts he had absorbed. The tears that ran down his face flowed just as freely as they had done when his left hand had ballooned in agony following his Olympic revenge over Steve McCrory in the same ring two years earlier.

After two rounds of hitting Callejas, Fenech returned to his corner with news that now it was his right hand that was busted.

He'd half expected that to happen. But he didn't expect it to hurt so much. Two weeks before in paradise he was taping his right hand with yards of extra bandage in a bid to hold it together for the biggest fight of his life. And when the fist betrayed him, he told Lewis that he would just have to go out for the rest of the bout and win the championship with his left.

Which he did with guts and gusto. Something he was keen to seize upon in his by now customary post-fight pat on the back before the adoring throng. Once the adrenalin rush had started to slow, the pain in Fenech's right hand started to hit harder than Callejas' left hook. When he grabbed the microphone, out came a distorted story about how his hand had been broken for a month, how he hadn't dared tell trainer Lewis and how history had been more important to him than the prospect of agony.

"I'm the first fighter in history to win three world titles with a broken hand," he roared, as Lewis waved his arms frantically, trying to quieten his champion. Once Fenech was up and running he was hard to stop, he had been hard to hit with a legal blow. Everybody left the Entertainment Centre suitably impressed.

Fenech had given the newspapers, the closed circuit telecasters and the radio broadcasters, a great story. Not only had he made history, but he had done so single-handedly, as it were. Not only had he performed a miracle, but he had done it as though one hand had been tied behind his back.

Carl King, the manager of Azumah Nelson and son of the gregarious fight promoter Don King, left for his office in New York, tallying the dollars a fight between Fenech and Nelson would generate.

Twelve thousand people left the Entertainment Centre having seen a far better fight than Fenech's warm-up bout, a 56-second blast out of Argentina's world-rated featherweight Osmar Avila on December 11.

Victor Callejas left with a terrible headache and a terrible feeling of failure. He had tried everything to slow Fenech down, but even a one-handed adversary was more than he could handle.

Fenech left the Entertainment Centre and headed for the nearest Maserati dealership, stopping off to become embroiled in a brief political storm over his damaged fist.

In the middle of a NSW State election campaign that displayed almost as many dirty tricks as Victor Callejas, Fenech claimed he'd been denied adequate treatment at two public hospitals, something the Liberal opposition was keen to pounce upon as a weapon against the Labor Government.

Then there were allegations from the Unsworth Government that Fenech had been used as a political pawn by Dr Bruce Shepherd, the Liberal stalwart and surgeon who had remedied Fenech's troubled left fist in 1986.

It was just another example of the fact that Fenech can't please all the people all the time. In fact, he can't please some of the people even some of the time.

No matter how many world titles he wins, how many records he breaks, how many jaws he fractures, how many faces he hits, he will always have his detractors and enemies. It is simply the nature of the beast and the form of his battleground.

Not everyone in Australia likes Jeff Fenech, but many people idolise him, many more respect him and some even fear him.

Boxers and boxing don't appeal to every Australian and that's probably a good thing. But Jeff Fenech is rich and famous and drives a car that costs about double that of the average Australian home.

And he gets paid a lot of money to let out all his aggression on victims, who despite their obvious credentials, end up looking like lambs to the slaughter after a couple of minutes of close-up combat.

To a tough little street punk who had nothing but his wits six years ago, getting paid a fortune to belt people is paradise.

Heaven on earth. ∎

23
Winners And Losers

*"If I should meet some of my friends on the
street the next morning after I have lost a
fight, they'll be searching for holes in the
pavement"*

> Gunboat Smith,
> heavyweight contender, 1914.

When Gentleman Jim Corbett proved that the great John L. Sullivan was no longer able to lick any man in the house, as the first world heavyweight boxing champion was apt to boast, he set a trend that endures to this day in a sport, which like no other, devours its great ones as quickly as it spawns them.

There are no niceties in boxing. Great champions rarely bow out like great tennis players or cricketers or golfers. Some, like Joe Louis, farewell the sport from the canvas, victims of some younger monster, climbing over prone bodies to the top. Some, like Muhammad Ali, become so dependent on public adulation that they allow themselves to be lured back again and again to the sacrificial altar. Some, like Sugar Ray Robinson, make enough money from a single bout to live the rest of their lives in luxury, but are still fighting in their old age, distorted shadows of their glory days. Others, like Davey Moore, Benny Paret and Deuk Koo Kim leave boxing in the back of a hearse.

Rocky Graziano once said: "Fighting is the only racket where you're almost guaranteed to end up as a bum."

Gentleman Jim, the handsome dandy once described as "the father of modern boxing", brought fast footwork and counter-punching to a sport previously dominated by oafish brawlers. In tarnishing the fame of the great John L. he set the precedent for thousands of sad career finales in boxing. He helped frame the odds which suggest that Jeff Fenech, by all the laws of probability, must suffer some form of humiliating setback before his retirement.

Nearly every great champion has stuck around for one fight too many. It's virtually inevitable. Nearly all of them from John L. down to Richie Sandoval to Samart Payakarun and Carlos Zarate have gone out of the sport that made them celebrities, the sad way. Broken men whose time at the top was no cushion for the fall from grace.

Jim Corbett stuck around for too long and was knocked out by Bob Fitzsimmons, who was still fighting at the age of 52 and died broke. Fitzsimmons was knocked out by Jim Jeffries who was lured from a six-year retirement and made boxing's Great White Hope only to be mocked and mutilated by Jack Johnson, the first black heavyweight champion who laughed at the stumbling, bewildered, bloodied man all the way to the bank. In turn, Johnson was persecuted for his love of white women and his hatred of white men until Kansas farm boy Jess Willard flattened him under the Havana sun. Years after he, in turn, had been all but killed by Jack Dempsey, years after Dempsey had hit him so hard that Willard finished their fight with his jaw-bone jutting through the flesh of his cheek, the humble giant admitted that he had always hated boxing "as I never hated a thing previously". But there was money in it.

Joe Louis, ravaged by taxes and age, was slaughtered by Rocky Marciano (who later died in a plane crash) after 25 defences of his world heavyweight title. In later years Louis became a cripple, wheeled out to fights at the Las Vegas casino where he worked as a greeter — a patronised ghost of glories past. He suffered from delusions, too, and for a time believed that the Mafia was trying to kill him with poisoned gas. His wife called it "the most pathetic thing in the world".

Muhammad Ali may have been the best known man on earth. He was the fastest, the prettiest, the most colourful, charismatic and controversial heavyweight champion in history. He became an inspiration for the downtrodden everywhere, especially the black man. More than anyone else he made self-confidence an art form. In his prime he publicly prayed for the day when he could walk around unnoticed. But he found retirement unfulfilling. And lonely. At the age of 38 and after being convinced by Larry Holmes and Trevor Berbick that he was no longer The Greatest and after years of driving around Los Angeles in an open Rolls Royce so the multitudes would still acknowledge him, Ali became a figure for boxing abolitionists to point to as proof. His speech became slurred, his face bloated and his hurricane speed stilled. Dave Anderson of the New York Times called Ali's exit from boxing, a stumble into the sunset.

In turn Holmes and Berbick both suffered the cruellest forms of defeat. Holmes twice lost to a light-heavyweight, Michael Spinks, when he was on the verge of topping Marciano's all-time record for victories. Berbick was left reeling like a legless duck against Mike Tyson. Tyson later ended Holmes' brief comeback with a crushing knockout.

Even before he flew to Los Angeles for the Olympics, Fenech's intention had been to get out of boxing while he was still a young man. To make a few quick kills, buy a house or two or three, own a nice, fast sports car and have money in the bank. He always wanted to retire to a life where he could do nothing more challenging than watch football and see his investments prosper.

It's an old formula and, like old fighters, it usually fails.

Willie Pep was faster and smarter than Fenech. He was one of the greatest of all featherweights and maybe the most glorious defensive genius boxing has known. At the age of 42 he was still fighting. Famous columnist Jimmy Cannon likened him to a hoofer suddenly gone deaf and missing the orchestra's beat.

"I guess you'd like to know what happened to all the big money," Pep once sighed. "So would I. I've piled up so much scar tissue that I look like I'm wearing blinders. But boxing is my business. Only way I know how to make so much so fast."

At another time Pep summed up the demise of a fighter this way: "First your legs go. Then you lose your reflexes. Then you lose your friends."

They coined the phrase "pound for pound" just for Sugar Ray Robinson because, pound for pound, he was the greatest fistfighter who ever lived. At the peak of his prosperity he travelled the world with a barber, a chauffeur, a valet, a secretary, a golf pro and the usual entourage of floosies and flunkies. He once owned several blocks of Harlem real estate and many New York businesses. But he lost most of his money and was still fighting at the age of 45 for pitiful purses in pitiful places. His manager George Gainford could only despair: "Oh my God. Look at this man. He can do nothing, anymore".

"I never had a day's pleasure out of fighting in my life," said Sugar Ray, "I wanted to quit at the top, but you cannot choose your endings anymore than your beginnings. We been winners. We been losers.

"A while back I used to love to fight, now it's strictly business. Fights remind me of the old barbaric days when people used to fight in a pit, while other people threw them money."

Boxers are like that. Fighters start out hooked on the thrilling high of combat. Then they get addicted to the bright lights. Then it all becomes a callous business.

"I'm after the big money like the rest," British heavyweight Brian London once remarked. "Anybody who says he likes boxing needs his brain tested."

Boxers spend their youth clawing and slashing and brawling their way to the top. Once there the mere thought of living outside the spotlight, trapped in the darkness of defeat, terrifies them into clinging on. Defeat scares them more than any opponent.

As heavyweight champ Floyd Patterson, a man who knew all about the pain and loneliness of defeat, once explained: "The losing fighter loses more than just his pride and the fight; he loses part of the future, he is one step closer to the slums he came from."

Boxing by its very nature breeds strong, courageous admirable men. But also venal scum.

Primo Carnera was the greatest patsy of all time. A lumbering, bumbling mountain of a man.

Paul Gallico described him as "a helpless lamb among wolves, who used him until there was nothing more left to use, until the last possible penny had been squeezed from his big carcass, and then abandoned him". A victim of the seedy, greedy, vicious, conniving element of boxing that has always existed to prey upon it like jackals.

Randolph Turpin, the pride of England, made half a million dollars from a single fight with Ray Robinson in the '50s, when half a million dollars was really something. A few years later he was nothing more than a sideshow freak, a carnival wrestler with shades of Quasimodo. He killed himself when the pressure of just living became too great.

In his book Sports in America, James A. Michener quotes a survey: "S. Kirson Weinberg and Harry Arnold compiled an analysis of what happened to 90 former boxing champions, each of whom had earned more than $100,000 in years when that amount of money was substantial and when there were few taxes. They now worked in taverns, or as unskilled labourers, or as ticket takers at movie houses, or as bookies, or as janitors, or as helpers around gas stations, or as men walking racehorses. Not one had a substantial job."

Closer to home there are the tragedies of Lionel Rose, Elley Bennett, Ron Richards and Young Griffo, all champions who ended up dead broke, Trevor Thornberry, who ended up broken and Chuck Wilburn, who ended up dead.

Of course there have been success stories. But most are tainted. Gene Tunney quit at the peak of his profession, but America never forgave him for beating Jack Dempsey. Max Schmeling became the Coca-Cola king of West Germany, but has never been able to forget the dreadful night Joe Louis literally broke his back with a body punch. Even Sugar Ray Leonard, for all his millions, suffered defeat against Roberto Duran.

Every time a champion loses, it is further evidence of the diminishing chances of any fighter, Fenech included, retiring unbeaten and with their faculties and wealth intact.

Before the second Shingaki fight, Fenech boasted of how he wanted to maim the diffident Japanese and show him the other side of Australian hospitality. In the years to come the chances are that some hotshot streetfighter from the slums of Mexico City or the barrios of Panama will predict some similar fate for the Marrickville Mauler and then set about ending his career.

It would be the kind of stumbling exit with which Fenech would find difficulty coping. Already he has considered the grim prospect of defeat many times. Often the spectre of failure has kept him awake, tossing restlessly and agitated in his bed.

"I guess there's always someone somewhere who can shock you," he admits, a little ruefully, "Maybe someone really, really quick — like a souped-up version of Coffee — might be able to jab and run for 15 rounds and beat me on points. But I doubt it. I think Lewie has me too fit for anyone to get away from me for the whole distance. I guess a big puncher would have the best chance. Not because I'm weak on the chin or anything like that, but because the only way I'd ever stop throwing punches back is if I was out cold. I don't think anyone could keep away from me for 15 rounds.

"If I did lose I'd retire. I'd like the chance to fight the bloke who beat me a second time and if I couldn't win I'd give the fight game a miss. Boxing at my level is only good if you're the best. If you're second rate you end up a stepping stone for someone else. Or worse."

Cocky, but always aware.

The notion of defeat, the concept of being a victim in someone else's rise to the top, is odious to a boxer. But it is a notion which lurks in every fighter's consciousness with the rise of every unbeaten prospect, the advent of each young knockout sensation and the news of each stunning upset.

The law of averages says that Fenech must lose sometime and that he cannot retire from one of the riskiest of all businesses rich and happy. Shortly before he won the IBF junior-lightweight title, the profession of Barry Michael was summed up by his father and co-trainer Len Swettenham. He reasoned that boxing was merely the exchange of brain cells for money. That every time a boxer took a solid blow to the head he lost a part, however miniscule, of his intellectual capacity. The sole aim of professional boxing from his son's point of view, he said, was to make sure the profits were greater than the pains.

John Lewis says his job, since Fenech first came into his gymnasium, has been to minimise the risks and maximise the rewards. In effect, to beat the law of averages.

"All along I maintained that there wasn't much future for anyone in boxing unless they could capture the public imagination," Lewis said. "Unless they were pretty damned good. When you boil it down to its most simple form, boxing is a rotten business. It's full of blokes so mean they'd skin a cockroach. Sometimes I wonder what I'm doing mixed up in it all. But boxing has done great things for Jeff. When he first started training I made it my job to see that boxing made Jeff Fenech a better person. He hasn't always done the right thing, but I'm proud of what he became.

"He is the most loyal kid in the world. He would die to save a friend. But he can also be the cruellest, most terrifying, most vicious person alive. He used to take out his frustrations on other kids in the street, now he saves it for the ring. His personality is pretty much the same as ever, but fortunately, society only gets to see the darker side of him now when it's all legal.

"Now that Jeff is at the top, after all we've been though

together, it's my job to see that he finishes on top. If I don't believe he can win a fight I'll pull him out of it. Jeff only fights when I believe he can win. Even if it meant giving up whatever title he holds at that time. I wouldn't hesitate to cancel a fight. He means too much to me to take any chances. People can get killed in boxing."

Fortunately Fenech has not yet had to face the repugnant reality of death in the ring and, hopefully, he never will. But death has haunted him in other ways. Death has never been far away but it has only succeeded in catching those close to him. Death and dying have been a haunting part of Fenech's life since Paul's heart gave out while his son was still in the womb. Fenech's father almost died on the eve of the Shingaki rematch and before the Greg Richardson walkover. His heart stopped for good two months after the Callejas fight. And before several crucial periods in his career three of Fenech's closest friends died — one a suicide, another electrocuted at work and the third from a heart attack. They were all young men, a fact that made the grieving all the more profound. There have been so many tragedies. Losing his one chance to become Australia's first gold medallist in Olympic boxing was shattering too, but only a hiccup by comparison.

Fenech's family soars with elation one day and weeps and wails the next. That has been the pattern of their unpredictable existence since Paul and Mary dodged the bombs and the bullets as children. You would think they would be prepared for anything.

But shortly after Fenech's knockout of McCrory, his family was rocked as never before. The eldest son Godfrey, an enigmatic loner as a kid, had been arrested and charged with the murder of a 19-year-old apprentice panel beater, Luke Robertson. A week before the Richardson fight, Godfrey was sentenced to life in prison. The pain to the rest of the Fenech family, still unconditioned to upheaval despite the frequency with which it struck, was numbing.

Jeff Fenech kept a brave public face, but privately he was shattered. For the first time in a life that had become dependent on support from the media, he was chasing reporters and news crews from his home.

And the hate mail poured in from that peculiar element of Australian society that hates to see anyone, especially some "little bloody wog", kick on. Much of it came from the same misanthropes who write to him before every fight expressing a shared prayer that he die in the ring.

With Godfrey in jail and on the front page of every newspaper in Australia and with Jeff facing extensive surgery and perhaps even premature retirement after the McCrory bout because of his injured hand, the world champion was in the worst spirits ever.

But he remained a fighter in the truest sense. Anyone who could use boxing as a medium to gain a nation's respect at a time when the fight game was on its last legs in this country, has to have special qualities. And it is those qualities, Fenech's inner strength, the sheer drive, the will-power that is both frightening and inspiring to behold, the heart and the guidance of Lewis, that may let him leave boxing the way he has always planned. With his head up.

Fenech's attitude to a lifestyle he would not otherwise have known, swings appreciably, depending on his mood at any given time. After beating Coffee he said he wanted to quit in a year and lap up the good life. After Payakarun he was talking about winning a world record four titles with the featherweight and junior-lightweight crowns still to come. So big an attraction would he become, he claimed, that they would have to hold his fights at some place "really big" like the Sydney Cricket Ground.

At other times he would lament the pressures of fame. How there were so many people out there waiting for him to fall. How people would pick fights with him for no other reason than to embarrass him in the press.

When his mood is low, Fenech will say he'd like to get out of boxing right now and punch on with every mug who wants to tackle him in a nightclub or disco. Only the prospect of headlines restrains him. Many times he has claimed that he will never miss boxing. Like Muhammad Ali more than 20 years before, he has been known to publicly pray for the day when he can walk around unnoticed. Yet, such talk is a contradiction for a man who sometimes seems lost without the public adulation.

Lewis plays down Fenech's talk of retirement.

"He loves the fame and attention. Boxing has brought him so much that I don't think he could let go of the spotlight without a fight. Sometimes I think he'd be lost without all the publicity. I guess that's the trap with any kind of public success. My biggest aim with Jeff is that he will leave boxing when I tell him it's time. He's listened to me ever since he met me. I hope he is still listening when I tell him to hang up the gloves.

"The kid is pretty well set up with houses and money in the bank and I reckon he'll finish up okay. He's just too cunning to let his money slip through his fingers."

Fenech has been cunning enough to make himself one of the most admired of all Australians. He has made no advancements in medical research, certainly made no contributions to world peace, did nothing much to alleviate starvation in the Third World and devised no political manifesto. But he gave a nation a hero. The only thing he is really good at is bashing people up. Yet he probably made more fans than Joan Sutherland and Patrick White put together.

His rise from the streets to glitter status was pure Hollywood in a setting to which every Australian could relate. But there was also more to his success than just another story of the underdog beating the odds.

In a sport, which many say is no sport at all, only senseless, legalised brutality, an anachronism we could all do without, Fenech used boxing as the medium through which he could sell himself and his talent. It was a medium that has been both revered and reviled since its birth with the Ancient Greeks 3500 years ago.

"Why does boxing arouse so much outrage and passionate defence?" Ronald Levao, a New York academic, asks in *The Ring* . "Spectators from all social levels, aware of its brutality and corruption, are likewise drawn to boxing with a fascination wholly unlike the campy, carnivalesque slumming that marks the recent boom in professional wrestling. There is too, the mysterious appeal of boxing to masters of literary narrative, from Homer to Virgil to Hemingway and Mailer. Perhaps the spectacle's very marginality makes it irresistable.

"Its violent action seems at once senseless and self-sufficient, beyond the reach of any possible translation ... something gratuitous, yet fundamental, a vivid and candid enactment of all struggle."

Writing in Time magazine, A.N. Maiden said: "No doubt Fenech causes many Australians to ponder similar questions. He is a throwback, an uncomfortable reminder of a harsher past that may be in all our futures. But on fight night, he will draw an audience like a magnet."

Boxing arouses the full spectrum of emotions from its faithful. The same people who stood to applaud the courage of

Shingaki in his first fight with Fenech were screaming for his blood in the second. The same people who admire Fenech's fortitude and charm can just as easily implore his evil side to emerge.

"Even the spectator who dislikes violence in principle," wrote Joyce Carol Oates, "Can come to admire highly skilled boxing — to admire it beyond all 'sane' proportions. A brilliant boxing match, quicksilver in its motions, transpiring far more rapidly than the mind can absorb, can have the power that Emily Dickinson attributed to great poetry: you know it's great when it takes the top of your head off. (The physical imagery Dickinson employs is peculiarly apt in this context)."

Boxing became Fenech's saviour, not just financially, emotionally and socially. In the profound words of Levao it became Fenech's way of expressing a genius that might otherwise have remained unexpressed, perhaps inexpressable.

Within months of turning tragedy into triumph after Los Angeles, Fenech had made himself the most successful athlete in Australia during a time when the national cricket team was battling Sri Lanka to climb from the bottom of the international ladder, a time before Greg Norman's assault on every major golf tournament in the world and when Wimbledon was only a dream for Pat Cash. Fenech was what the Australian public wanted. He was a winner. Put him in with anyone from anywhere and he would come away with his arms raised. He was proving to the world, at least that part of the world interested in boxing, that Australian - made was as good as anything from overseas. ■

24
Standing Tall

"I've been all around the world . . . met ambassadors, presidents. Boxing made me important. A little cockroach crawling around the ghetto. Now I'm important. Break my jaw and I still got my million dollars."

Hector Camacho,
world lightweight champion, 1986.

Fenech's achievements in the boxing ring, despite their necessary brutality, despite their frequent dependency on the worst aspects of human nature, have made him a hero and an inspiration. He is both brave and beastly, determined and deadly.

While the very forum for his fame is constantly threatened with abolition, Fenech transcends boxing. Charity organisations love to be associated with him, old ladies, who know not the difference between a left hook and a Liverpool Kiss, queue for his autograph. He may be capable of dark and terrifying violence in the heat of battle, but to most Australians he is the kid who got up off his backside and had a go. Living proof of Joe Frazier's belief that man is capable of anything if he tries hard enough.

From the time he first laced up a pair of boxing gloves, Fenech realised his natural aggression and inherent athleticism represented his only crack at the bright lights. He realised that through boxing he could become bigger, stronger, tougher and more admired than he could through any other medium.

John Lewis made Fenech a champion and Fenech did his best to make Lewis proud. He is still hot-blooded, still willing to punch on with anyone who insults his trainer or his mates, or merely cuts him off in the traffic. He says he will always be quick-tempered because that is his nature. But he also says boxing made and mellowed him.

Where would Fenech be without boxing? Perhaps he was talented and tough enough to have played rugby league for Australia. He was certainly daring and impetuous enough to have ended up with a bullet between his eyes. Or in a jail cell with a number on his back.

But by 1988 Fenech had achieved more than any other fighter from anywhere ever, in such a short period. Within six years and eight months of his first impromptu session with Mark Cribb and his first meeting with John Lewis, Fenech had been an Australian amateur champion and had fought with distinction at the Olympic Games. More to the point, he had become the only Australian ever to win two world professional titles and one of only 11 men in boxing history to hold three. After crushing Victor Callejas for his triple crown, he had his steely eyes set on championships four and five.

He had achieved it all without any of the more dramatic injuries that have given boxing such a black and blue image with medical authorities all over the world. His nose, first broken by a children's plastic spade, and his hands rebuilt with a surgeon's scalpel, were the only real signs that he made his living beating up people — with society's blessing.

He is rich and famous enough to enjoy first-name privileges with the prime minister of Australia.

And he has carried Australian boxing to such an extent that to paraphrase Muhammad Ali, boxing in this country will probably be nothing again when he's gone.

When he was a teenager Fenech developed the same dim view of human nature that 60 years ago befell the ascetic fictional hero created in Sinclair Lewis' masterpiece, Arrowsmith.

During a time of acute despair and frustration, Arrowsmith laments with emptied illusions: "All wise men are bandits. They're loyal to their friends, but they despise the rest".

Fenech is still loyal to his friends, fiercely protective, but he no longer hates the rest of society. In boxing he has achieved what he set out to win, most conspicuously, respect for a little guy in a big man's world.

Fenech is a dozen different people in one. He is a romantic and a chauvinist, he can run for hours in stifling plastic sweatsuits yet can be so lazy that he would drive to the gym just 50 metres from his front door. He is the prototype contradiction. A cunning businessman and a soft touch. He can be brutal and as cold-blooded as a death adder, yet he adores Con Spyropoulos, a poor simple soul he protects like a baby. He can be disarmingly honest and subtly devious. He is brave and strong and tough, but as vulnerable to emotion as an adolescent schoolgirl. He says he hates publicity, but would most likely wither without it.

When the American jockey Eddie Arcaro was once quizzed on possible retirement, he said he would stay in the saddle for as long as he could. Away from the winner's circle, he would be just be another little guy waiting for a table in a restaurant.

Jeff Fenech will always be a little guy, but even in retirement, whether he bows out with arms high or his head buried in his hands, he will be much more than a little guy waiting on the whim of a maitre'd.

Ever since he was 15, Fenech has been five feet seven trying to be six feet three. In boxing he became so much taller than that. The little guy made some big dreams come true. ■

THE PROFESSIONAL RECORD OF
JEFF FENECH

1984

Oct 12	KO 2	Bobby Williams	Sydney
Oct 26	KO 7	Percy Israel	Sydney
Nov 30	KO 4	Junior Thompson	Sydney
		(Wins Australian super-flyweight title)	
Dec 15	KO 2	Ilesa Manila	Suva, Fiji

1985

Feb 1	KO 5	Wayne Mulholland	Dapto
		(Wins NSW and South Pacific bantamweight titles)	
Mar 4	KO 4	Rolly Navarro	Sydney
Apr 26	KO 9	Satoshi Shingaki	Sydney
		(Wins IBF bantamweight title)	
Jun 14	KO 6	John Matienza	Sydney
Jly 26	KO 9	John Farrell	Brisbane
Aug 23	KO 3	Satoshi Shingaki	Sydney
		(Retains IBF title)	
Nov 4	KO 2	Kenny Butts	Brisbane
Dec 2	W15	Jerome Coffee	Sydney
		(Retains IBF title)	

1986

Apr 11	W10	Daniel Zaragoza	Perth
Jly 18	KO 14	Steve McCrory	Sydney
		(Retains IBF title)	

1987

Apr 3	W12	Tony Miller	Melbourne
		(Wins Australian featherweight title)	
May 8	KO 4	Samart Payakarun	Sydney
		(Wins WBC super-bantamweight title)	
Jly 10	KO 5	Greg Richardson	Sydney
		(Retains WBC title)	
Oct 16	WTD 4	Carlos Zarate	Sydney
		(Retains WBC title)	
Dec 11	KO 1	Osmar Avila	Sydney

1988

| Mar 7 | KO 10 | Victor Callejas | Sydney |
| | | (Wins WBC featherweight title) | |

LEGEND:
KO = knockout
W = points decision
TD = technical decision